———⊷⊶———

GOD'S ANSWERS
FOR YOUR
EVERY QUESTION

———⊷⊶———

**ALBURY
PUBLISHING**
TULSA, OKLAHOMA

2nd Printing

God's Answers for Your Every Question

ISBN 1-57778-093-0
Copyright © 1998 by ALBURY PUBLISHING
P.O. Box 470406
Tulsa, Oklahoma 74147-0406

CONTENTS

HOW CAN I KNOW YOU, GOD?

LORD, I NEED SOME ADVICE.
CAN YOU HELP ME?

Table of Contents

LORD, WHAT'S THE SECRET TO GOOD RELATIONSHIPS?

———◇◇◇———

Q: SO MUCH HAS CHANGED
SINCE THE BIBLE WAS WRITTEN.
HOW CAN I BE SURE ITS ANSWERS
STILL APPLY TO MY LIFE TODAY?

———◇◇◇———

A: Even if it was written in Scripture long
ago, you can be sure it's written for us.

ROMANS 15:4 THE MESSAGE

Every Scripture is God-breathed — given by
His inspiration.

2 TIMOTHY 3:16 AMP

"I tell you the truth, until heaven and earth
disappear, not the smallest letter, not the least
stroke of a pen, will by any means disappear
from the Law until everything is accomplished."

MATTHEW 5:18 NIV

"People are like grass that dies away; their beauty fades as quickly as the beauty of wildflowers.
The grass withers, and the flowers fall away. But
the word of the Lord will last forever."

1 PETER 1:24,25 NLT

Every part of Scripture is...useful one way or another — showing us truth, exposing our rebellion, correcting our mistakes, training us to live God's way.

2 TIMOTHY 3:16 THE MESSAGE

The word of God is living and powerful.

HEBREWS 4:12 NKJV

They are not just idle words for you — they are your life.

DEUTERONOMY 32:47 NIV

PRAYERS

Open my eyes to see the wonderful truths in your law.

PSALM 119:18 NLT

Forever, O Lord, your word stands firm in heaven. Your faithfulness extends to every generation, as enduring as the earth you created. Your laws remain true today, for everything serves your plans.

PSALM 119:89-91 NLT

From studying your laws, I found out long ago that you made them to last forever. All you say can be trusted; your teachings are true and will last forever.

PSALM 119:152,160 CEV

PROMISES

The law of the Lord is perfect, reviving the soul. The decrees of the Lord are trustworthy, making wise the simple. The commandments of the Lord are right, bringing joy to the heart. The commands of the Lord are clear, giving insight to life.

The laws of the Lord are true; each one is fair. They are more desirable than gold, even the finest gold. They are sweeter than honey, even honey dripping from the comb. They are a warning to those who hear them; there is great reward for those who obey them.

PSALM 19:7-11 NLT

"Heaven and earth will pass away, but My words will not pass away."

MATTHEW 24:35 NASB

Q: I BELIEVE IN GOD AND I GO
TO CHURCH. IS THAT ENOUGH...
OR IS THERE MORE?

A: He...said, Men, what is it necessary for me to do that I may be saved?

And they answered, Believe in and on the Lord Jesus Christ — that is, give yourself up to Him, take yourself out of your own keeping and entrust yourself into His keeping, and you will be saved.

ACTS 16:30,31 AMP

Jesus replied, "I assure you, unless you are born again, you can never see the Kingdom of God."

"What do you mean?" exclaimed Nicodemus. "How can an old man go back into his mother's womb and be born again?"

Jesus replied, "The truth is, no one can enter the Kingdom of God without being born of water and the Spirit. Humans can reproduce only human life, but the Holy Spirit gives new life from heaven."

JOHN 3:3-6 NLT

For God so greatly loved and dearly prized the world that He [even] gave up His only-begotten (unique) Son, so that whoever believes in (trusts, clings to, relies on) Him shall not perish — come to destruction, be lost — but have eternal (everlasting) life.

JOHN 3:16 AMP

Anyone who trusts in him is acquitted; anyone who refuses to trust him has long since been under the death sentence without knowing it. And why? Because of that person's failure to believe in the one-of-a-kind Son of God when introduced to him.

JOHN 3:18 THE MESSAGE

And all who trust him — God's Son — to save them have eternal life.

JOHN 3:36 TLB

For if you do not believe that I am He [Who I claim to be] — if you do not adhere to, trust in and rely on Me — you will die in your sins.

JOHN 8:24 AMP

Q: JESUS, I WANT TO BELIEVE IN
YOU. HOW CAN I BE SURE YOU
ARE REALLY REAL?

A: You will seek Me, inquire for and require
Me [as a vital necessity] and find Me; when
you search for Me with all your heart, I will be
found by you, says the Lord.

JEREMIAH 29:13,14 AMP

"For everyone who asks receives, and he who
seeks finds, and to him who knocks it will be
opened."

MATTHEW 7:8 NASB

All who seek the Lord will praise him. Their
hearts will rejoice with everlasting joy.

PSALM 22:26 NLT

The person who has My commands and keeps
them is the one who [really] loves Me, and
whoever [really] loves Me will be loved by My
Father. And I [too] will love him and will
show (reveal, manifest) Myself to him — I will

let Myself be clearly seen by him and make
Myself real to him.

JOHN 14:21 AMP

INSTRUCTIONS

Before you trust, you have to listen. But unless
Christ's Word is preached, there's nothing to
listen to.

ROMANS 10:17 THE MESSAGE

For what I received I passed on to you as of
first importance: that Christ died for our sins
according to the Scriptures, that he was buried,
that he was raised on the third day according
to the Scriptures, and that he appeared to
Peter, and then to the Twelve. After that, he
appeared to more than five hundred of the
brothers at the same time

1 CORINTHIANS 15:3-6 NIV

To these He also presented Himself alive after
His suffering, by many convincing proofs,
appearing to them over a period of forty days
and speaking of the things concerning the
kingdom of God.

ACTS 1:3 NASB

There are also many other things that Jesus
did, which if they were written one by one, I

suppose that even the world itself could not contain the books that would be written.

JOHN 21:25 NKJV

These have been written so that you may believe that Jesus is the Christ, the Son of God; and that believing you may have life in His name.

JOHN 20:31 NASB

For you know that God paid a ransom to save you from the empty life you inherited from your ancestors. And the ransom he paid was not mere gold or silver. He paid for you with the precious lifeblood of Christ, the sinless, spotless Lamb of God. God chose him for this purpose long before the world began, but now in these final days, he was sent to the earth for all to see. And he did this for you.

Through Christ you have come to trust in God. And because God raised Christ from the dead and gave him great glory, your faith and hope can be placed confidently in God.

For you have been born again. Your new life did not come from your earthly parents because the life they gave you will end in death. But this new life will last forever because it comes from the eternal, living word of God.

1 Peter 1:18-21,23 NLT

Can you imagine the breathtaking recovery life makes, sovereign life, in those who grasp with both hands this wildly extravagant life-gift, this grand setting-everything-right, that the one man Jesus Christ provides? Here it is in a nutshell: Just as one person [Adam] did it wrong and got us in all this trouble with sin and death, another person did it right and got us out of it. But more than just getting us out of trouble, he got us into life!

Romans 5:17,18 the message

PROMISES

He is real and...he rewards those who truly want to find him.

Hebrews 11:6 NCV

"No one's ever seen or heard anything like this, never so much as imagined anything quite like it — what God has arranged for those who love him." But you've seen and heard it because God by his Spirit has brought it all out into the open before you.

We didn't learn this by reading books or going to school; we learned it from God, who taught us person-to-person through Jesus, and we're passing it on to you in the same first-hand, personal way.

The unspiritual self, just as it is by nature, can't receive the gifts of God's Spirit. There's no capacity for them. They seem like so much silliness. Spirit can be known only by spirit — God's Spirit and our spirits in open communion.

1 CORINTHIANS 2:9,13-15 THE MESSAGE

God once said, "Let the light shine out of the darkness!" This is the same God who made his light shine in our hearts by letting us know the glory of God that is in the face of Christ.

2 CORINTHIANS 4:6 NCV

PRAYERS

I pray for you constantly, asking God, the glorious Father of our Lord Jesus Christ, to give you wisdom to see clearly and really understand who Christ is and all that he has done for you. I pray that your hearts will be flooded with light so that you can see something of the future he has called you to share.... I pray that you will begin to understand how incredibly great his power is to help those who believe him.

EPHESIANS 1:17-19 TLB

Hear my voice when I call, O Lord; be merciful to me and answer me. My heart says of you, "Seek his face!" Your face, Lord, I will seek.

PSALM 27:7,8 NIV

EXAMPLE

"Doubting Thomas" said he had to see for himself that Jesus was alive (John 20:24,25). Jesus appeared to him and said:

"Put your finger here; see my hands. Reach out your hand and put it into my side. Stop doubting and believe." Thomas said to him, "My Lord and my God!"

JOHN 20:27,28 NIV

Jesus said, "So, you believe because you've seen with your own eyes. Even better blessings are in store for those who believe without seeing."

JOHN 20:29 THE MESSAGE

Q: IS THERE SOMETHING
I NEED TO DO TO BEGIN
A RELATIONSHIP WITH
YOU, LORD? HOW DO
I GET STARTED?

A: Salvation that comes from trusting
Christ...is already within easy reach. In fact,
the Scriptures say, "The message is close at
hand; it is on your lips and in your heart."
For if you confess with your mouth that Jesus
is Lord and believe in your heart that God
raised him from the dead, you will be saved.
For it is by believing in your heart that you are
made right with God, and it is by confessing
with your mouth that you are saved. As the
Scriptures tell us, "Anyone who believes in him
will not be disappointed."
                                    ROMANS 10:8-11 NLT

"The word that saves is right here, as near as
the tongue in your mouth, as close as the
heart in your chest." It's the word of faith that

welcomes God to go to work and set things
right for us.

ROMANS 10:8 THE MESSAGE

PROMISES

To all who believed him and accepted him, he
gave the right to become children of God.
They are reborn! This is not a physical birth
resulting from human passion or plan — this
rebirth comes from God.

JOHN 1:12,13 NLT

Therefore, if anyone is in Christ, he is a new
creation; old things have passed away; behold,
all things have become new.

2 CORINTHIANS 5:17 NKJV

God our Savior showed us how good and kind
he is. He saved us because of his mercy, and
not because of any good things that we have
done. God washed us by the power of the
Holy Spirit. He gave us new birth and a fresh
beginning. God sent Jesus Christ our Savior to
give us his Spirit. Jesus treated us much better
than we deserve. He made us acceptable to
God and gave us the hope of eternal life.

TITUS 3:4-7 CEV

If we say we have fellowship with God, but we continue living in darkness, we are liars and do not follow the truth. But if we live in the light, as God is in the light, we can share fellowship with each other. Then the blood of Jesus, God's Son, cleanses us from every sin.

If we say we have no sin, we are fooling ourselves, and the truth is not in us. But if we confess our sins, he will forgive our sins, because we can trust God to do what is right. He will cleanse us from all the wrongs we have done.

1 JOHN 1:6-9 NCV

PRAYERS

Say the welcoming word to God — "Jesus is my Master" — embracing, body and soul, God's work of doing in us what he did in raising Jesus from the dead. That's it. You're not "doing" anything; you're simply calling out to God, trusting him to do it for you. That's salvation. With your whole being you embrace God setting things right, and then you say it, right out loud: "God has set everything right between him and me!"

ROMANS 10:9,10 THE MESSAGE

Q: God, the Bible calls You our Father in Heaven. How are You like a father to me?

A: He surrounds me with lovingkindness and tender mercies. He fills my life with good things!

PSALM 103:4,5 TLB

The Lord is merciful and gracious; he is slow to get angry and full of unfailing love. He will not constantly accuse us, nor remain angry forever. He has not punished us for all our sins, nor does he deal with us as we deserve. For his unfailing love toward those who fear him is as great as the height of the heavens above the earth. He has removed our rebellious acts as far away from us as the east is from the west.

The Lord is like a father to his children, tender and compassionate to those who fear him. For he understands how weak we are; he knows we are only dust.

PSALM 103:8-14 NLT

Whatever is good and perfect comes to us from God above, who created all heaven's lights. Unlike them, he never changes or casts shifting shadows. In his goodness he chose to make us his own children by giving us his true word. And we, out of all creation, became his choice possession.

JAMES 1:17,18 NLT

If God gives such attention to the appearance of wildflowers — most of which are never even seen — don't you think he'll attend to you, take pride in you, do his best for you?

MATTHEW 6:30 THE MESSAGE

I will instruct you and teach you in the way which you should go; I will counsel you with My eye upon you.

PSALM 32:8 NASB

Your ears shall hear a word behind you, saying, "This is the way, walk in it," whenever you turn to the right hand or whenever you turn to the left.

ISAIAH 30:21 NKJV

"The Lord corrects the people he loves and disciplines those he calls his own."

HEBREWS 12:6 CEV

The Father is a merciful God, who always gives us comfort. He comforts us when we are in trouble, so that we can share that same comfort with others in trouble.

2 CORINTHIANS 1:3,4 CEV

And we have known and believed the love that God has for us. God is love. We love Him because He first loved us.

1 JOHN 4:16,19 NKJV

We used to be stupid, disobedient, and foolish, as well as slaves of all sorts of desires and pleasures. We were evil and jealous. Everyone hated us, and we hated everyone. God our Savior showed us how good and kind he is. He saved us because of his mercy, and not because of any good things that we have done. God washed us by the power of the Holy Spirit. He gave us new birth and a fresh beginning. God sent Jesus Christ our Savior to give us his Spirit.

TITUS 3:3-6 CEV

It was all his doing; we had nothing to do with it. He gave us a good bath, and we came out of it new people, washed inside and out by the Holy Spirit.

TITUS 3:4-7 THE MESSAGE

PROMISES

"For the eyes of the Lord run to and fro throughout the whole earth, to show Himself strong on behalf of those whose heart is loyal to Him."

2 CHRONICLES 16:9 NKJV

He is a rewarder of those who diligently seek Him.

HEBREWS 11:6 NKJV

The Lord is faithful, and He will strengthen and protect you from the evil one.

2 THESSALONIANS 3:3 NASB

"As a mother comforts her child, so will I comfort you."

ISAIAH 66:13 NIV

And therefore the Lord [earnestly] waits — expectant, looking and longing — to be gracious to you, and therefore He lifts Himself up that He may have mercy on you and show loving-kindness to you...Blessed — happy, fortunate [to be envied] are all those who [earnestly] wait for Him, who expect and look and long for Him [for His victory, His favor, His love, His peace, His joy and His matchless, unbroken companionship].... He will surely be gracious to you at the sound of your cry; when He hears it, He will answer you.

ISAIAH 30:18,19 AMP

"Can a mother forget the baby at her breast and have no compassion on the child she has borne? Though she may forget, I will not forget you! See, I have engraved you on the palms of my hands."

ISAIAH 49:15,16 NIV

"They will be mine," says the Lord Almighty, "in the day when I make up my treasured possession. I will spare them, just as in compassion a man spares his son who serves him.

MALACHI 3:17 NIV

"The Lord your God in your midst, The Mighty One, will save; He will rejoice over you with gladness, He will quiet you with His love, He will rejoice over you with singing."

ZEPHANIAH 3:17 NKJV

The Lord is gracious and compassionate, slow to anger and rich in love. The Lord is good to all; he has compassion on all he has made.

PSALM 145:8,9 NIV

———❖———

Q: I KNOW ABOUT GOD THE
FATHER AND HAVE RECEIVED
JESUS AS MY SAVIOR. WHAT'S THE
HOLY SPIRIT'S ROLE IN MY LIFE?

———❖———

A: I will give you a new heart and put a
new spirit in you; I will remove from you your
heart of stone and give you a heart of flesh.
And I will put my Spirit in you and move you
to follow my decrees and be careful to keep my
laws.

EZEKIEL 36:26,27 NIV

INSTRUCTIONS

He washed away our sins and gave us a new
life through the Holy Spirit. He generously
poured out the Spirit upon us because of what
Jesus Christ our Savior did.

TITUS 3:5,6 NLT

The name of our Lord Jesus Christ and the
power of God's Spirit have washed you and

made you holy and acceptable to God.

1 CORINTHIANS 6:11 CEV

The power of the life-giving Spirit has freed you through Christ Jesus from the power of sin that leads to death.

ROMANS 8:2 NLT

When I think of the wisdom and scope of God's plan, I fall to my knees and pray to the Father, the Creator of everything in heaven and on earth. I pray that from his glorious, unlimited resources he will give you mighty inner strength through his Holy Spirit.

EPHESIANS 3:14-16 NLT

You should behave...like God's very own children, adopted into his family — calling him "Father, dear Father." For his Holy Spirit speaks to us deep in our hearts and tells us that we are God's children. And since we are his children, we will share his treasures — for everything God gives to his Son, Christ, is ours, too.

ROMANS 8:15-17 NLT

When the Holy Spirit controls our lives, he will produce this kind of fruit in us: love, joy, peace, patience, kindness, goodness, faithfulness, gentleness, and self-control.

GALATIANS 5:22,23 NLT

The Friend, the Holy Spirit whom the Father
will send at my request, will make everything
plain to you. He will remind you of all the
things I have told you.

JOHN 14:26 THE MESSAGE

Jesus said to his disciples: If you love me, you
will do as I command. Then I will ask the
Father to send you the Holy Spirit who will
help you and always be with you. The Spirit
will show you what is true. The people of this
world cannot accept the Spirit, because they
don't see or know him. But you know the
Spirit, who is with you and will keep on living
in you.

JOHN 14:15-17 CEV

The Spirit shows what is true and will come
and guide you into the full truth. The Spirit
doesn't speak on his own. He will tell you only
what he has heard from me, and he will let you
know what is going to happen.

JOHN 16:13 CEV

When the Comforter (Counselor, Helper,
Advocate, Intercessor, Strengthener) comes

Whom I will send to you from the Father, the
Spirit of Truth Who comes (proceeds) from the
Father, He [Himself] will testify regarding Me.

JOHN 15:26 AMP

As it is written in the Scriptures: "No one has
ever seen this, and no one has ever heard about
it. No one has ever imagined what God has
prepared for those who love him." But God
has shown us these things through the Spirit.

The Spirit searches out all things, even the
deep secrets of God. Who knows the thoughts
that another person has? Only a person's spirit
that lives within him knows his thoughts. It is
the same with God. No one knows the
thoughts of God except the Spirit of God.
Now we did not receive the spirit of the world,
but we received the Spirit that is from God so
that we can know all that God has given us.

1 CORINTHIANS 2:9-12 NCV

Those who trust God's action in them find
that God's Spirit is in them — living and
breathing God!

ROMANS 8:5 THE MESSAGE

The Holy Spirit helps us in our distress. For
we don't even know what we should pray for,

nor how we should pray. But the Holy Spirit prays for us with groanings that cannot be expressed in words. And the Father who knows all hearts knows what the Spirit is saying, for the Spirit pleads for us believers in harmony with God's own will.

ROMANS 8:26,27 NLT

Dear friends, use your most holy faith to build yourselves up, praying in the Holy Spirit.

JUDE 20 NCV

Pray in the Spirit at all times with all kinds of prayers, asking for everything you need.

EPHESIANS 6:18 NCV

On the final and climactic day of the Feast, Jesus took his stand. He cried out, "If anyone thirsts, let him come to me and drink. Rivers of living water will brim and spill out of the depths of anyone who believes in me this way, just as the Scripture says." (He said this in regard to the Spirit, whom those who believed in him were about to receive. The Spirit had not yet been given because Jesus had not yet been glorified.)

JOHN 7:37-39 THE MESSAGE

He gave them this command: "Do not leave

Jerusalem, but wait for the gift my Father promised, which you have heard me speak about. For John baptized with water, but in a few days you will be baptized with the Holy Spirit."

ACTS 1:4,5 NIV

"You will receive power when the Holy Spirit comes on you; and you will be my witnesses in Jerusalem, and in all Judea and Samaria, and to the ends of the earth."

ACTS 1:8 NIV

And everyone present was filled with the Holy Spirit and began speaking in languages they didn't know, for the Holy Spirit gave them this ability.

ACTS 2:4 TLB

Then Peter stepped forward with the eleven other apostles and shouted to the crowd... "What you see this morning was predicted centuries ago by the prophet Joel:

'In the last days, God said, I will pour out my Spirit upon all people. Your sons and your daughters will prophesy, your young men will see visions, and your old men will dream dreams. In those days I will pour out my Spirit upon all my servants, men and women alike, and they will prophesy.'"

ACTS 2:14,16-18 NLT

"Jesus was lifted up to heaven and is now at God's right side. The Father has given the Holy Spirit to Jesus as he promised. So Jesus has poured out that Spirit, and this is what you now see and hear."

ACTS 2:33 NCV

Peter said to them, "Change your hearts and lives and be baptized, each one of you, in the name of Jesus Christ for the forgiveness of your sins. And you will receive the gift of the Holy Spirit. This promise is for you, for your children, and for all who are far away. It is for everyone the Lord our God calls to himself."

ACTS 2:38,39 NCV

While Peter was still speaking these words, the Holy Spirit came on all who heard the message. The circumcised believers who had come with Peter were astonished that the gift of the Holy Spirit had been poured out even on the Gentiles. For they heard them speaking in tongues and praising God. Then Peter said, "Can anyone keep these people from being baptized with water? They have received the

Holy Spirit just as we have." ACTS 10:44-47 NIV

When Paul placed his hands on them, the Holy Spirit came on them, and they spoke in tongues and prophesied. ACTS 19:6 NIV

Don't be drunk with wine, because that will ruin your life. Instead, let the Holy Spirit fill and control you. Then you will sing psalms and hymns and spiritual songs among yourselves, making music to the Lord in your hearts. And you will always give thanks for everything to God the Father in the name of our Lord Jesus Christ. EPHESIANS 5:18-20 NLT

Q: HOW CAN I
PLEASE YOU, GOD?

A: Then one of the scribes...asked Him, "Which is the first commandment of all?"

Jesus answered him, "The first of all the commandments is: 'Hear, O Israel, the Lord our God, the Lord is one. And you shall love the Lord your God with all your heart, with all your soul, with all your mind, and with all your strength.' This is the first commandment. "And the second, like it, is this: 'You shall love your neighbor as yourself.' There is no other commandment greater than these."

MARK 12:28-31 NKJV

The Lord delights in those who fear him, who put their hope in his unfailing love.

PSALM 147:11 NIV

"God is Spirit, and those who worship Him must worship in spirit and truth."

JOHN 4:24 NKJV

"That's the kind of people the Father is out looking for: those who are simply and honestly themselves before him in their worship...Those who worship him must do it out of their very being, their spirits, their true selves, in adoration."

JOHN 4:23,24 THE MESSAGE

INSTRUCTIONS

Give unto the Lord the glory due to His name; worship the Lord in the beauty of holiness.

PSALM 29:2 NKJV

Rejoice always, pray without ceasing, in everything give thanks; for this is the will of God in Christ Jesus for you.

1 THESSALONIANS 5:16-18 NKJV

Sing, sing your hearts out to God! Let every detail in your lives — words, actions, whatever — be done in the name of the Master, Jesus, thanking God the Father every step of the way.

COLOSSIANS 3:17 THE MESSAGE

Celebrate God all day, every day. I mean, revel

in him! Don't fret or worry. Instead of worry-ing, pray. Let petitions and praises shape your worries into prayers, letting God know your concerns. Before you know it, a sense of God's wholeness, everything coming together for good, will come and settle you down. It's won-derful what happens when Christ displaces worry at the center of your life.

PHILIPPIANS 4:4,6,7 THE MESSAGE

Trust in Him at all times, O people; pour out your heart before Him; God is a refuge for us. Selah.

PSALM 62:8 NASB

Fix these words of mine in your hearts and minds...Teach them to your children, talking about them when you sit at home and when you walk along the road, when you lie down and when you get up.

DEUTERONOMY 11:18,19 NIV

Every part of Scripture is God-breathed and useful one way or another — showing us truth, exposing our rebellion, correcting our mistakes, training us to live God's way.

2 TIMOTHY 3:16 THE MESSAGE

PRAYERS

May God, who puts all things together, makes all things whole...Now put you together, provide you with everything you need to please him, make us into what gives him most pleasure, by means of the sacrifice of Jesus, the Messiah.

HEBREWS 13:20,21 THE MESSAGE

May the words of my mouth and the meditation of my heart be pleasing in your sight, O Lord, my Rock and my Redeemer.

PSALM 19:14 NIV

EXAMPLE

David was a man who pleased the Lord. In fact, the Bible gives him this commendation:

"I've searched the land and found this David, son of Jesse. He's a man whose heart beats to my heart, a man who will do what I tell him."

ACTS 13:22 THE MESSAGE

What was David's "secret"? He understood and enjoyed the grace of God. He had deep love and respect for the Lord and a great desire to express that love in worship:

God — you're my God! I can't get enough of you! I've worked up such hunger and thirst for God, traveling across dry and weary deserts. So here I am in the place of worship, eyes open, drinking in your strength and glory. In your generous love I am really living at last! My lips brim praises like fountains. I bless you every time I take a breath; my arms wave like banners of praise to you.

PSALM 63:1-4 THE MESSAGE

Thank you! Everything in me says "Thank you!" Angels listen as I sing my thanks. I kneel in worship facing your holy temple and say it again: "Thank you!" Thank you for your love, thank you for your faithfulness.

PSALM 138:1,2 THE MESSAGE

---❖---

Q: I JUST BLEW IT AGAIN, LORD. ARE YOU SURE I'M STILL SAVED?

---❖---

A: In the past all of us lived like them, trying to please our sinful selves and doing all the things our bodies and minds wanted. We should have suffered God's anger because of the way we were.... But God's mercy is great, and he loved us very much. Though we were spiritually dead because of the things we did against God, he gave us new life with Christ. You have been saved by God's grace.

EPHESIANS 2:3-5 NCV

INSTRUCTIONS

You have been saved by grace through believing. You did not save yourselves; it was a gift from God. It was not the result of your own efforts, so you cannot brag about it.

EPHESIANS 2:8,9 NCV

It is clear, then, that God's promise... [was based on] the new relationship with God that comes by faith. So if you claim that God's promise is for those who obey God's law and think they are "good enough" in God's sight, then you are saying that faith is useless. And in that case, the promise is also meaningless....

Faith is the key! God's promise is given to us as a free gift. And we are certain to receive it...if we have faith like Abraham's.

ROMANS 4:13,14,16 NLT

Can't you see the central issue in all this? It is not what you and I do.... It is what God is doing, and he is creating something totally new, a free life!

GALATIANS 6:15 THE MESSAGE

PROMISES

The fulfillment of God's promise depends entirely on trusting God and his way, and then simply embracing him and what he does. God's promise arrives as pure gift. That's the only way everyone can be sure to get in on it.

ROMANS 4:16 THE MESSAGE

God has given us eternal life, and this life is in
His Son. He who has the Son has life; he who
does not have the Son of God does not have
life. These things I have written to you who
believe in the name of the Son of God, that
you may know that you have eternal life, and
that you may continue to believe in the name
of the Son of God.

1 JOHN 5:11-13 NKJV

Yet to all who received him, to those who
believed in his name, he gave the right to
become children of God.

JOHN 1:12 NIV

I tell you the truth, whoever hears what I say
and believes in the One who sent me has eternal life. That person will not be judged guilty
but has already left death and entered life.

JOHN 5:24 NCV

Anyone here who...aligns himself with the
Father, who has in fact put me in charge, has at
this very moment the real, lasting life.

JOHN 5:24 THE MESSAGE

"My sheep hear My voice, and I know them,
and they follow Me; and I give eternal life to

them, and they shall never perish; and no one
shall snatch them out of My hand."

JOHN 10:27,28 NASB

For it is God Who is all the while effectually
at work in you — energizing and creating in
you the power and desire — both to will and
to work for His good pleasure and satisfaction
and delight.

PHILIPPIANS 2:13 AMP

I will lead the blind by ways they have not
known...I will turn the darkness into light
before them and make the rough places
smooth. These are the things I will do; I will
not forsake them.

ISAIAH 42:16 NIV

By entering through faith into what God has
always wanted to do for us — set us right with
him, make us fit for him — we have it all
together with God because of our Master
Jesus. And that's not all: We throw open our
doors to God and discover at the same
moment that he has already thrown open his
door to us. We find ourselves standing where
we always hoped we might stand — out in the
wide open spaces of God's grace and glory,

standing tall and shouting our praise.

ROMANS 5:1-3 THE MESSAGE

And you shall know — with an acquaintance and understanding based on and grounded in personal experience — that I am the Lord: for they shall not be put to shame who wait for, look for, hope for and expect Me.... For thus says the Lord, Even the captives of the mighty shall be taken away, and the prey of the terrible shall be delivered; for I will contend with him who contends with you.

ISAIAH 49:23,25 AMP

For He Himself has said, "I will never leave you nor forsake you."

HEBREWS 13:5 NKJV

PRAYER

I pray for you constantly, asking God, the glorious Father of our Lord Jesus Christ, to give you wisdom to see clearly and really understand who Christ is and all that he has done for you. I pray that your hearts will be flooded with light so that you can see something of the future he has called you to share.... I pray that you will begin to understand how incredibly

great his power is to help those who believe
him. It is that same mighty power That raised
Christ from the dead and seated him in the
place of honor at God's right hand in heaven.

EPHESIANS 1:16-20 TLB

EXAMPLE

*Abraham received right standing with God by
faith, apart from any good works that he did. The
Bible calls him the "father of all people who
embrace what God does for them"* (ROMANS 4:11
THE MESSAGE).

Abraham never wavered in believing God's
promise.... He was absolutely convinced that
God was able to do anything he promised.

ROMANS 4:20,21 NLT

When everything was hopeless, Abraham
believed anyway, deciding to live not on the
basis of what he saw he couldn't do but on
what God said he would do.... He didn't tiptoe
around God's promise asking cautiously skepti-
cal questions. He plunged into the promise and
came up strong, ready for God, sure that God

would make good on what he had said. That's
why it is said, "Abraham was declared fit before
God by trusting God to set him right."

ROMANS 4:17,20-22 THE MESSAGE

Now this wonderful truth — that God
declared him to be righteous — wasn't just for
Abraham's benefit. It was for us, too, assuring
us that God will also declare us to be righteous
if we believe in God, who brought Jesus our
Lord back from the dead. He was handed over
to die because of our sins, and he was raised
from the dead to make us right with God.

ROMANS 4:23-25 NLT

Q: WHAT ABOUT PRAYER?
IS THERE A CERTAIN WAY
I SHOULD PRAY TO YOU?

A: "This is what I want you to do: Ask the Father for whatever is in keeping with the things I've revealed to you. Ask in my name, according to my will, and he'll most certainly give it to you."

JOHN 16:23,24 THE MESSAGE

INSTRUCTIONS

Keep on asking, and you will be given what you ask for. Keep on looking, and you will find. Keep on knocking, and the door will be opened. For everyone who asks, receives. Everyone who seeks, finds. And the door is opened to everyone who knocks. You parents — if your children ask for a loaf of bread, do you give them a stone instead? Or if they ask for a fish, do you give them a snake? Of course not! If you sinful people know how to give good gifts to your children, how much more will your heavenly Father give good gifts to those who ask him.

MATTHEW 7:7-11 NLT

I am the vine, and you are the branches. If you stay joined to me, and I stay joined to you, then you will produce lots of fruit. But you cannot do anything without me. Stay joined to me and let my teachings become part of you. Then you can pray for whatever you want, and your prayer will be answered.

JOHN 15:5,7 CEV

God is strong, and he wants you strong. So take everything the Master has set out for you, well-made weapons of the best materials. And put them to use so you will be able to stand up to everything the Devil throws your way. This is no afternoon athletic contest that we'll walk away from and forget about in a couple of hours. This is for keeps, a life-or-death fight to the finish against the Devil and all his angels.

Be prepared. You're up against far more than you can handle on your own. Take all the help you can get, every weapon God has issued, so that when it's all over but the shouting you'll still be on your feet.... God's Word is an *indispensable* weapon. In the same way, prayer is essential in this ongoing warfare. Pray hard and long.

EPHESIANS 6:10-18 THE MESSAGE

Never give up praying. And when you pray, keep alert and be thankful.

COLOSSIANS 4:2 CEV

Always pray by the power of the Spirit.

EPHESIANS 6:18 CEV

The Holy Spirit helps us in our distress. For we don't even know what we should pray for, nor how we should pray. But the Holy Spirit prays for us with groanings that cannot be expressed in words. And the Father who knows all hearts knows what the Spirit is saying, for the Spirit pleads for us believers in harmony with God's own will.

ROMANS 8:26,27 NLT

I will pray with the spirit, and I will also pray with the understanding.

1 CORINTHIANS 14:15 NKJV

PROMISES

The LORD is near to all who call upon Him, to all who call upon Him in truth. He will fulfill the desire of those who fear Him; He will also hear their cry and will save them.

PSALM 145:18,19 NASB

The eyes of the Lord are on the righteous, and His ears are open to their cry.... The righteous cry out, and the Lord hears, and delivers them out of all their troubles.

PSALM 34:15,17 NKJV

"Before they call, I will answer; and while they are still speaking, I will hear."

ISAIAH 65:24 NKJV

Then said the Lord to me...I am alert and active, watching over My word to perform it.

JEREMIAH 1:12 AMP

This is the confidence which we have before Him, that, if we ask anything according to His will, He hears us. And if we know that He hears us in whatever we ask, we know that we have the requests which we have asked from Him.

1 JOHN 5:14,15 NASB

"Again, I tell you that if two of you on earth agree about anything you ask for, it will be done for you by my Father in heaven. For where two or three come together in my name, there am I with them."

MATTHEW 18:19,20 NIV

And Jesus replying said to them, Have faith in God (constantly). Truly, I tell you, whoever says to this mountain, Be lifted up and thrown into the sea! and does not doubt at all in his heart, but believes that what he says will take place, it will be done for him. For this reason I am telling you, whatever you ask for in prayer, believe — trust and be confident — that it is granted to you, and you will [get it].

MARK 11:22-24 AMP

Let us then fearlessly and confidently and boldly draw near to the throne of grace...that we may receive mercy...and find grace to help in good time for every need — appropriate help and well-timed help, coming just when we need it.

HEBREWS 4:16 AMP

The earnest (heartfelt, continued) prayer of a righteous man makes tremendous power available — dynamic in its working.

JAMES 5:16 AMP

With God's power working in us, God can do

much, much more than anything we can ask or
imagine.

EPHESIANS 3:20 NCV

PRAYERS

I pray that Christ will live in your hearts by
faith and that your life will be strong in love and
be built on love. And I pray that you...will have
the power to understand the greatness of
Christ's love — how wide and how long and
how high and how deep that love is. Christ's
love is greater than anyone can ever know, but I
pray that you will be able to know that love.
Then you can be filled with the fullness of God.

EPHESIANS 3:17-19 NCV

We ask God to give you a complete understanding of what he wants to do in your lives,
and we ask him to make you wise with spiritual
wisdom. Then the way you live will always
honor and please the Lord, and you will continually do good, kind things for others...We also
pray that you will be strengthened with his glorious power so that you will have all the patience
and endurance you need. May you be filled with
joy, always thanking the Father.

COLOSSIANS 1:9-12 NLT

Q: LORD, SO MANY
DECISIONS FACE ME DAILY —
WHERE CAN I TURN FOR
DIRECTION AND GUIDANCE?

A: If you need wisdom — if you want to
know what God wants you to do — ask him,
and he will gladly tell you.

JAMES 1:5 NLT

INSTRUCTIONS

Call to me and I will answer you and tell you
great and unsearchable things you do not know.

JEREMIAH 33:3 NIV

My child, listen to me and treasure my
instructions. Tune your ears to wisdom, and
concentrate on understanding.... Search for
them as you would for lost money or hidden
treasure. Then you will understand what it
means to fear the Lord, and you will gain
knowledge of God.

PROVERBS 2:1,2,4,5 NLT

Trust God from the bottom of your heart.
Don't try to figure out everything on your own.
Listen for God's voice in everything you do,
everywhere you go. He's the one who will keep
you on track. Don't assume that you know it
all. Run to God!

PROVERBS 3:5-7 THE MESSAGE

All Scripture is inspired by God and is useful
to teach us what is true and to make us realize
what is wrong in our lives. It straightens us out
and teaches us to do what is right. It is God's
way of preparing us in every way, fully equipped
for every good thing God wants us to do.

2 TIMOTHY 3:16,17 NLT

PROMISES

I will instruct you and teach you in the way
you should go; I will counsel you and watch
over you.

PSALM 32:8 NIV

Your word is a lamp to my feet and a light to
my path.

PSALM 119:105 NKJV

The statutes of the Lord are trustworthy, making wise the simple. The precepts of the Lord

are right, giving joy to the heart. The commands of the Lord are radiant, giving light to the eyes. By them is your servant warned; in keeping them there is great reward.

PSALM 19:7,8,11 NIV

PRAYERS

Send forth your light and your truth, let them guide me.

PSALM 43:3 NIV

Show me the path where I should walk, O Lord; point out the right road for me to follow. Lead me by your truth and teach me, for you are the God who saves me. All day long I put my hope in you.

PSALM 25:4,5 NLT

Teach me to do your will, for you are my God. May your gracious Spirit lead me forward on a firm footing.

PSALM 143:10 NLT

"Give me an understanding mind so that I can govern your people well and know the difference between what is right and what is wrong. For who by himself is able to carry such a heavy responsibility?"

1 KINGS 3:9 TLB

I will bless the Lord who guides me; even at night my heart instructs me.

PSALM 16:7 NLT

Your statutes are my delight; they are my counselors.

PSALM 119:24 NIV

EXAMPLE

When an enemy army came against Jehoshaphat, he sought the Lord for wisdom and guidance:

"We have no power to face this vast army that is attacking us. We do not know what to do, but our eyes are upon you." Then the Spirit of the Lord came upon Jahaziel.... He said..."This is what the Lord says to you: 'Do not be afraid or discouraged because of this vast army. For the battle is not yours, but God's. Go out to face them tomorrow, and the Lord will be with you.'"

2 CHRONICLES 20:12,14,15,17 NIV

Q: LORD, I CAN'T SEEM TO STOP
WORRYING. IS THERE A WAY TO
FIND PEACE OF MIND?

A: Don't fret or worry. Instead of worrying,
pray. Let petitions and praises shape your worries into prayers, letting God know your concerns. Before you know it, a sense of God's
wholeness, everything coming together for
good, will come and settle you down. It's wonderful what happens when Christ displaces
worry at the center of your life.

PHILIPPIANS 4:6-8 THE MESSAGE

INSTRUCTIONS

Cast your burden on the Lord, and He shall
sustain you; He shall never permit the righteous to be moved.

PSALM 55:22 NKJV

Casting the whole of your care — all your anx-
ieties, all your worries, all your concerns, once

and for all — on Him; for He cares for you affectionately, and cares about you watchfully.

1 PETER 5:7 AMP

PROMISES

I am leaving you with a gift — peace of mind and heart. And the peace I give isn't like the peace the world gives. So don't be troubled or afraid.

JOHN 14:27 NLT

The Lord is my light and my salvation; whom shall I fear or dread? The Lord is the refuge and stronghold of my life; of whom shall I be afraid?

PSALM 27:1 AMP

In righteousness you shall be established; you shall be far from oppression, for you shall not fear; and from terror, for it shall not come near you.

ISAIAH 54:14 NKJV

Those who live in the shelter of the Most High will find rest in the shadow of the Almighty. This I declare of the Lord: He alone is my refuge, my place of safety; he is my God, and I am trusting him.

PSALM 91:1,2 NLT

You are my hiding place; you will protect me from trouble and surround me with songs of deliverance. Selah.

PSALM 32:7 NIV

For he will rescue you from every trap and protect you from the fatal plague. He will shield you with his wings.... His faithful promises are your armor and protection. Do not be afraid of the terrors of the night, nor fear the dangers of the day.... Though a thousand fall at your side, though ten thousand are dying around you, these evils will not touch you. For he orders his angels to protect you wherever you go.

PSALM 91:3-5,7,11 NLT

The Lord says, "I will rescue those who love me. I will protect those who trust in my name. When they call on me, I will answer; I will be with them in trouble. I will rescue them and honor them. I will satisfy them with a long life and give them my salvation."

PSALM 91:14-16 NLT

But the Lord is faithful, and he will strengthen and protect you from the evil one.

2 THESSALONIANS 3:3 NIV

The angel of the Lord encamps around those who fear Him, and rescues them.

PSALM 34:7 NASB

PRAYERS

May the God of hope fill you with all joy and peace as you trust in him, so that you may overflow with hope by the power of the Holy Spirit.

ROMANS 15:13 NIV

In the multitude of my (anxious) thoughts within me, Your comforts cheer and delight my soul!

PSALM 94:19 AMP

EXAMPLE

During the night of the first Passover, God protected His people. As they trusted and obeyed Him, they were kept safe.

Then Moses summoned all the elders of Israel and said to them, "Go at once and...slaughter the Passover lamb. Take a bunch of hyssop, dip it into the blood in the basin and put some of the blood on the top and on both sides of the doorframe. Not one of you shall go out the door of his house until morning. When the Lord goes through the land...he will see the blood...and will pass over that doorway, and he will not permit the destroyer to enter your houses and strike you down."

EXODUS 12:21-23 NIV

———◇———

Q: I WANT MY LIFE TO COUNT.
HOW CAN I REACH MY
FULL POTENTIAL?

———◇———

A: "It's not possible for a person to succeed
— I'm talking about eternal success — without
heaven's help."

JOHN 3:27 THE MESSAGE

Unless the Lord builds the house, they labor
in vain who build it; unless the Lord guards
the city, the watchman keeps awake in vain.

PSALM 127:1 NASB

O Lord my God...Your plans for us are too
numerous to list. If I tried to recite all your
wonderful deeds, I would never come to the
end of them.

PSALM 40:5 NLT

INSTRUCTIONS

In his heart a man plans his course, but the
Lord determines his steps.

PROVERBS 16:9 NIV

We humans keep brainstorming options and plans, but God's purpose prevails.

PROVERBS 19:21 THE MESSAGE

You're blessed when you stay on course, walking steadily on the road revealed by God. You're blessed when you follow his directions, doing your best to find him. That's right — you don't go off on your own; you walk straight along the road he set.

PSALM 119:1-3 THE MESSAGE

Devote yourselves to prayer with an alert mind and a thankful heart.

COLOSSIANS 4:2 NLT

"This book of the law shall not depart from your mouth, but you shall meditate on it day and night, so that you may be careful to do according to all that is written in it; for then you will make your way prosperous, and then you will have success."

JOSHUA 1:8 NASB

"Be strong and do not give up, for your work will be rewarded."

2 CHRONICLES 15:7 NIV

The lazy person will not get what he wants. But a hard worker gets everything he wants.

PROVERBS 13:4 ICB

Refuse good advice and watch your plans fail; take good counsel and watch them succeed.

PROVERBS 15:22 THE MESSAGE

Form your purpose by asking for counsel, then carry it out using all the help you can get.

PROVERBS 20:18 THE MESSAGE

Do you see a man skilled in his work? That man will work for kings. He won't have to work for ordinary people. PROVERBS 22:29 ICB

A lazy life is an empty life.

PROVERBS 12:27 THE MESSAGE

"Whoever wants to be great must become a servant."

MATTHEW 20:26 THE MESSAGE

PROMISES

"For I know the plans I have for you," declares the Lord, "plans to prosper you and not to harm you, plans to give you hope and a future. Then you will call upon me and come and pray to me, and I will listen to you. You will seek me and find me when you seek me with all your heart."

JEREMIAH 29:11-13 NIV

God can pour on the blessings in astonishing ways so that you're ready for anything and everything.

2 CORINTHIANS 9:8 THE MESSAGE

I can do all things through Christ, because he gives me strength.

PHILIPPIANS 4:13 NCV

We are God's workmanship, created in Christ Jesus to do good works, which God prepared in advance for us to do.

EPHESIANS 2:10 NIV

PRAYERS

I pray for good fortune in everything you do, and for your good health — that your everyday affairs prosper, as well as your soul!

3 JOHN 2 THE MESSAGE

We pray for God's power to help you do all the good things that you hope to do and that your faith makes you want to do. Then...you will bring honor to the name of our Lord Jesus, and he will bring honor to you.

2 THESSALONIANS 1:11,12 CEV

May the God of peace...equip you with all you need for doing his will. May he produce in

you, through the power of Jesus Christ, all that
is pleasing to him.

HEBREWS 13:20,21 NLT

EXAMPLE

*God chose Solomon to build the temple in Jerusalem.
His father, King David, encouraged him again and
again, reminding him that the Lord would be with
him as he worked to fulfill God's plan for his life.*

David also said to Solomon his son, "Be strong
and courageous, and do the work. Do not be
afraid or discouraged, for the Lord God, my
God, is with you. He will not fail you or forsake
you until all the work for the service of the temple of the Lord is finished.

1 CHRONICLES 28:20 NIV

---⟡---

Q: NOTHING IS GOING RIGHT!
IS THERE A WAY TO KEEP MY JOY
NO MATTER WHAT HAPPENS?

---⟡---

A: You are my hiding place! You protect me from trouble, and you put songs in my heart.

PSALM 32:7 CEV

I was pushed back and about to fall, but the Lord helped me. The Lord is my strength and my song; he has become my salvation.

PSALM 118:13,14 NIV

INSTRUCTIONS

Let all who take refuge in you be glad; let them ever sing for joy. Spread your protection over them, that those who love your name may rejoice in you. For surely, O Lord, you bless the righteous; you surround them with your favor as with a shield.

PSALM 5:11,12 NIV

Let the godly rejoice. Let them be glad in

God's presence. Let them be filled with joy. Sing praises to God and to his name! Sing loud praises to him who rides the clouds. His name is the Lord — rejoice in his presence!

PSALM 68:3,4 NLT

Let the heavens rejoice, and let the earth be glad; and let them say among the nations, "The Lord reigns." Oh, give thanks to the Lord, for He is good! For His mercy endures forever.

1 CHRONICLES 16:31,34 NKJV

Celebrate God all day, every day. I mean, revel in him!

PHILIPPIANS 4:4 THE MESSAGE

Speak to each other with psalms, hymns, and spiritual songs, singing and making music in your hearts to the Lord. Always give thanks to God the Father for everything, in the name of our Lord Jesus Christ.

EPHESIANS 5:19,20 NCV

And you shall rejoice before the Lord your God in all that you undertake.

DEUTERONOMY 12:18 AMP

Do everything without complaining.

PHILIPPIANS 2:14 NCV

Dear brothers and sisters, whenever trouble comes your way, let it be an opportunity for joy. For when your faith is tested, your endurance has a chance to grow. So let it grow, for when your endurance is fully developed, you will be strong in character and ready for anything.

JAMES 1:2-4 NLT

Though you have not seen him, you love him; and even though you do not see him now, you believe in him and are filled with an inexpressible and glorious joy.

1 PETER 1:8 NIV

PRAYERS

I will sing to the Lord as long as I live; I will sing praise to my God while I have my being. May my meditation be sweet to Him; I will be glad in the Lord.

PSALM 104:33,34 NKJV

I will greatly rejoice in the Lord, my soul shall be joyful in my God; for He has clothed me with the garments of salvation, He has covered me with the robe of righteousness, as...a bride adorns herself with her jewels.

ISAIAH 61:10 NKJV

It is good to say, "Thank you" to the Lord, to sing praises to the God who is above all gods. Every morning tell him, "Thank you for your kindness," and every evening rejoice in all his faithfulness. You have done so much for me, O Lord. No wonder I am glad! I sing for joy.

PSALM 92:1,2,4 TLB

Why are you cast down, O my inner self? And why should you moan over me and be disquieted within me? Hope in God and wait expectantly for Him; for I shall yet praise Him, Who is the help of my [sad] countenance, and my God.

PSALM 43:5 AMP

PROMISES

Though a righteous man falls seven times, he rises again.

PROVERBS 24:16 NIV

Blessed, happy, to be envied is the man who is patient under trial and stands up under temptation, for when he has stood the test and been approved he will receive [the victor's] crown of life which God has promised to those who love Him.

JAMES 1:12 AMP

We also have joy with our troubles, because we know that these troubles produce patience. And patience produces character, and character produces hope. And this hope will never disappoint us, because God has poured out his love to fill our hearts.

ROMANS 5:3-5 NCV

EXAMPLE

Just after God warns him of an impending invasion, Habakkuk declares that his joy is not based on his circumstances but in his God:

Fig trees may not grow figs. There may be no grapes on the vines. There may be no olives growing on the trees. There may be no food growing in the fields. There may be no sheep in the pens. There may be no cattle in the barns. But I will still be glad in the Lord. I will rejoice in God my Savior. The Lord God gives me my strength.

HABAKKUK 3:17-19 ICB

Q: I HAVE MADE A TERRIBLE
MISTAKE, AND I FEEL SO GUILTY.
WHAT SHOULD I DO?

A: I'm glad...that you were jarred into turn-
ing things around. You let the distress bring
you to God, not drive you from him. The
result was all gain, no loss. Distress that drives
us to God does that. It turns us around. It gets
us back in the way of salvation. We never
regret that kind of pain. But those who let distress drive them away from God are full of
regrets, end up on a deathbed of regrets.

And now, isn't it wonderful all the ways in which
this distress has goaded you closer to God?
You're more alive, more concerned, more sensitive, more reverent, more human, more passionate, more responsible. Looked at from any angle,
you've come out of this with purity of heart.

2 CORINTHIANS 7:9-11 THE MESSAGE

Just see what this godly sorrow produced in

you!...You showed that you have done everything you could to make things right.

2 CORINTHIANS 7:11 NLT

INSTRUCTIONS

He who conceals his sins does not prosper,
but whoever confesses and renounces them
finds mercy.

PROVERBS 28:13 NIV

Blessed is he whose transgressions are forgiv-
en, whose sins are covered. Blessed is the man
whose sin the Lord does not count against
him.

PSALM 32:1,2 NIV

When I kept it all inside, my bones turned to
powder, my words became daylong groans. The
pressure never let up; all the juices of my life
dried up. Then I let it all out; I said, "I'll make
a clean breast of my failures to God."
Suddenly the pressure was gone — my guilt
dissolved, my sin disappeared.

PSALM 32:3-5 THE MESSAGE

Confess your sins to each other and pray for
each other so that you can live together whole
and healed. The prayer of a person living right

with God is something powerful to be reckoned with.

JAMES 5:16 THE MESSAGE

"Go, and I, even I, will be with your mouth, and teach you what you are to say."

EXODUS 4:12 NASB

PROMISES

Is anyone crying for help? God is listening, ready to rescue you. If your heart is broken, you'll find God right there.

PSALM 34:17,18 THE MESSAGE

He heals the heartbroken and bandages their wounds.

PSALM 147:3 THE MESSAGE

For thus says the high and lofty One Who inhabits eternity, Whose name is Holy: I dwell in the high and holy place, with him also who is of a thoroughly penitent and humble spirit, to revive the spirit of the humble, and to revive the heart of the thoroughly penitent — bruised with sorrow for sin.

ISAIAH 57:15 AMP

If we walk in the Light as He Himself is in the Light, we have fellowship with one another, and the blood of Jesus His Son cleanses us from all sin. If we say that we have no sin, we are deceiving ourselves and the truth is not in us. If we confess our sins, He is faithful and righteous to forgive us our sins and to cleanse us from all unrighteousness.

1 JOHN 1:7-9 NASB

For as high as the heavens are above the earth, so great is his love for those who fear him; as far as the east is from the west, so far has he removed our transgressions from us. As a father has compassion on his children, so the Lord has compassion on those who fear him.

PSALM 103:11-13 NIV

PRAYERS

Create in me a pure heart, O God, and renew a steadfast spirit within me.

PSALM 51:10 NIV

Have mercy on me, O God, according to your unfailing love; according to your great compassion blot out my transgressions. Wash away all my iniquity and cleanse me from my sin. For I know my transgressions, and my sin is always before me.

PSALM 51:1-3 NIV

Now may our Lord Jesus Christ Himself, and our God and Father, who has loved us and given us everlasting consolation and good hope by grace, comfort your hearts and establish you in every good word and work. The Lord is faithful, who will establish you and guard you from the evil one.

2 Thessalonians 2:16,17; 3:3 NKJV

EXAMPLE

King David is an example of a man who received God's forgiveness and then forgave himself:

I said, "I will confess my transgressions to the Lord," and You forgave the iniquity of my sin.... You are my hiding place; You shall preserve me from trouble; You shall surround me with songs of deliverance. Selah.... Be glad in the Lord and rejoice, you righteous; and shout for joy, all you upright in heart!

Psalm 32:5,7,11 NKJV

God's gift of righteousness was so real to David that he was able to once again see himself as one of the righteous, as one who was upright in heart. And the revelation of God's mercy made him shout for joy!

Q: I WANT TO BE A GOOD
CHRISTIAN, BUT I KEEP
MESSING UP. HELP ME, LORD!
HOW CAN I CHANGE?

A: God is working in you, giving you the
desire to obey him and the power to do what
pleases him.

PHILIPPIANS 2:13 NLT

We are God's masterpiece. He has created us
anew in Christ Jesus, so that we can do the
good things he planned for us long ago.

EPHESIANS 2:10 NLT

INSTRUCTIONS

"Everyone who hears these words of Mine and
acts on them, may be compared to a wise man
who built his house on the rock. And the rain
fell, and the floods came, and the winds blew
and slammed against that house; and yet it did
not fall, for it had been founded on the rock.

I KEEP MESSING UP.
HOW CAN I CHANGE?

Everyone who hears these words of Mine and does not act upon them, will be like a foolish man who built his house on the sand. The rain fell, and the floods came, and the winds blew and slammed against that house; and it fell and great was its fall."

MATTHEW 7:24-27 NASB

Faith comes by hearing, and hearing by the word of God.

ROMANS 10:17 NKJV

As newborn babes, desire the pure milk of the word, that you may grow thereby.

1 PETER 2:2 NKJV

For you have been born again not of seed which is perishable but imperishable, that is, through the living and enduring word of God.

1 PETER 1:23 NASB

All Scripture is given by God and is useful for teaching, for showing people what is wrong in their lives, for correcting faults, and for teaching how to live right. Using the Scriptures, the person who serves God will be capable, having all that is needed to do every good work.

2 TIMOTHY 3:16,17 NCV

77

And so, dear brothers and sisters, I plead with you to give your bodies to God. Let them be a living and holy sacrifice — the kind he will accept. When you think of what he has done for you, is this too much to ask? Don't copy the behavior and customs of this world, but let God transform you into a new person by changing the way you think. Then you will know what God wants you to do, and you will know how good and pleasing and perfect his will really is.

ROMANS 12:1,2 NLT

Do not merely listen to the word, and so deceive yourselves. Do what it says. Anyone who listens to the word but does not do what it says is like a man who looks at his face in a mirror and, after looking at himself, goes away and immediately forgets what he looks like. But the man who looks intently into the perfect law that gives freedom, and continues to do this, not forgetting what he has heard, but doing it — he will be blessed in what he does.

JAMES 1:22-25 NIV

"This Book of the Law shall not depart from your mouth, but you shall meditate in it day

and night, that you may observe to do according to all that is written in it. For then you will
make your way prosperous, and then you will
have good success."

JOSHUA 1:8 NKJV

PROMISES

If any person is (ingrafted) in Christ, the
Messiah, he is (a new creature altogether,) a
new creation; the old (previous moral and spiritual condition) has passed away. Behold, the
fresh and new has come!

2 CORINTHIANS 5:17 AMP

In the past you were slaves to sin — sin con-
trolled you. But thank God, you fully obeyed the
things that you were taught. You were made free
from sin, and now you are slaves to goodness.

ROMANS 6:17,18 NCV

And having been set free from sin, you have
become the servants of righteousness — of con-
formity to the divine will in thought, purpose
and action.

ROMANS 6:18 AMP

Such is the reliance and confidence that we
have through Christ... Not that we are fit

(qualified and sufficient in ability) of ourselves...
but our power and ability and sufficiency are
from God. [It is He] Who has qualified us
(making us to be fit and worthy and sufficient).

2 CORINTHIANS 3:4-6 AMP

God gives us what it takes to do all that we do.

2 CORINTHIANS 3:5 CEV

PRAYERS

We keep on praying for you that our God...
will make you as good as you wish you could
be! — rewarding your faith with his power.
Then everyone will be praising the name of the
Lord Jesus Christ because of the results they
see in you; and your greatest glory will be that
you belong to him. The tender mercy of our
God and of the Lord Jesus Christ has made all
this possible for you. 2 THESSALONIANS 1:11,12 TLB

We have kept on praying and asking God to
help you understand what he wants you to do;
asking him to make you wise about spiritual
things; and asking that the way you live will
always please the Lord and honor him, so that

you will always be doing good, kind things for others, while all the time you are learning to know God better and better. We are praying, too, that you will be filled with his mighty, glorious strength so that you can keep going no matter what happens — always full of the joy of the Lord.

COLOSSIANS 1:9-11 TLB

EXAMPLE

The Apostle Paul experienced a tremendous turn-around in his life after he believed on the Lord Jesus:

Even though I was once a blasphemer and a persecutor and a violent man, I was shown mercy because I acted in ignorance and unbelief. The grace of our Lord was poured out on me abundantly, along with the faith and love that are in Christ Jesus.

1 TIMOTHY 1:13,14 NIV

Jesus Christ came into the world to save sinners. I'm proof — Public Sinner Number One — of someone who could never have made it apart from sheer mercy. And now he shows me off — evidence of his endless patience — to those who are right on the edge of trusting him forever.

1 TIMOTHY 1:15,16 THE MESSAGE

Q: WHAT SHOULD I DO WHEN I'M TEMPTED TO SIN?

A: "I have set before you life and death, blessing and cursing; therefore choose life, that both you and your descendants may live; that you may love the Lord your God, that you may obey His voice, and that you may cling to Him, for He is your life."

DEUTERONOMY 30:19,20 NKJV

Remember this — the wrong desires that come into your life aren't anything new and different. Many others have faced exactly the same problems before you. And no temptation is irresistible. You can trust God to keep the temptation from becoming so strong that you can't stand up against it, for he has promised this and will do what he says. He will show you how to escape temptation's power so that you can bear up patiently against it.

1 CORINTHIANS 10:13 TLB

INSTRUCTIONS

Happy is the man who doesn't give in and do wrong when he is tempted, for afterwards he will get as his reward the crown of life that God has promised those who love him.

And remember, when someone wants to do wrong it is never God who is tempting him, for God never wants to do wrong and never tempts anyone else to do it. Temptation is the pull of man's own evil thoughts and wishes. These evil thoughts lead to evil actions.

JAMES 1:12-15 TLB

How blessed is the man who does not walk in the counsel of the wicked, nor stand in the path of sinners, nor sit in the seat of scoffers! But his delight is in the law of the Lord, and in His law he meditates day and night. And he will be like a tree firmly planted by streams of water, which yields its fruit in its season, and its leaf does not wither; and in whatever he does, he prospers.

PSALM 1:1-3 NASB

"If you want a happy life and good days, keep your tongue from speaking evil, and keep your lips from telling lies. Turn away from evil and do good. Work hard at living in peace with others. The eyes of the Lord watch over those who do right, and his ears are open to their prayers. But the Lord turns his face against those who do evil."

1 PETER 3:10-12 NLT

The good man does not escape all troubles — he has them too. But the Lord helps him in each and every one.

PSALM 34:19 TLB

The steps of good men are directed by the Lord. He delights in each step they take. If they fall it isn't fatal, for the Lord holds them with his hand.

PSALM 37:23,24 TLB

Be on your guard and stay awake. Your enemy, the devil, is like a roaring lion, sneaking around to find someone to attack. But you must resist the devil and stay strong in your faith.

1 PETER 5:8,9 CEV

Put on the full armor of God so that you can fight against the devil's evil tricks. Our fight is not against people on earth but...against the spiritual powers of evil in the heavenly world. That is why you need to put on God's full

armor. Then on the day of evil you will be able
to stand strong. And when you have finished
the whole fight, you will still be standing. So
stand strong, with the belt of truth tied around
your waist and the protection of right living on
your chest. On your feet wear the Good News
of peace.... And also use the shield of faith
with which you can stop all the burning arrows
of the Evil One. Accept God's salvation as
your helmet, and take the sword of the Spirit,
which is the word of God. Pray in the Spirit at
all times with all kinds of prayers.

EPHESIANS 6:11-18 NCV

You are strong, and the word of God lives in
you, and you have overcome the evil one.

1 JOHN 2:14 NIV

How we thank God, who gives us victory over
sin and death through Jesus Christ our Lord!

1 CORINTHIANS 15:57 NLT

For every child of God can obey him, defeat-
ing sin and evil pleasure by trusting Christ to
help him.

1 JOHN 5:4 TLB

Sin didn't and doesn't have a chance in

competition with the aggressive forgiveness we call grace. When it's sin versus grace, grace wins hands down. All sin can do is threaten us with death, and that's the end of it. Grace, because God is putting everything together again through the Messiah, invites us into life — a life that goes on and on and on, world without end.

ROMANS 5:20,21 THE MESSAGE

PROMISES

The Lord knows how to deliver the godly out of temptations.

2 PETER 2:9 NKJV

The Lord is faithful, and He will strengthen and protect you from the evil one.

2 THESSALONIANS 3:3 NASB

You are from God, little children, and have overcome them; because greater is He who is in you than he who is in the world.

1 JOHN 4:4 NASB

I can do everything with the help of Christ who gives me the strength I need.

PHILIPPIANS 4:13 NLT

God began doing a good work in you. And he
will continue it until it is finished when Jesus
Christ comes again. I am sure of that.

PHILIPPIANS 1:6 ICB

Now glory be to God! By his mighty power at
work within us, he is able to accomplish infinite-
ly more than we would ever dare to ask or hope.

EPHESIANS 3:20 NLT

God can do anything, you know — far more
than you could ever imagine or guess or
request in your wildest dreams! He does it not
by pushing us around but by working within
us, his Spirit deeply and gently within us.

EPHESIANS 3:20 THE MESSAGE

[Not in your own strength] for it is God
Who is all the while effectually at work in you
— energizing and creating in you the power
and desire — both to will and to work for His
good pleasure and satisfaction and delight.

PHILIPPIANS 2:13 AMP

Anyone who meets a testing challenge head-
on and manages to stick it out is mighty fortunate. For such persons loyally in love with

God, the reward is life and more life.

JAMES 1:12 THE MESSAGE

I know how great this makes you feel, even though you have to put up with every kind of aggravation in the meantime. Pure gold put in the fire comes out of it proved pure; genuine faith put through this suffering comes out proved genuine. When Jesus wraps this all up, it's your faith, not your gold, that God will have on display as evidence of his victory.

1 PETER 1:6,7 THE MESSAGE

These trials are only to test your faith, to see whether or not it is strong and pure. It is being tested as fire tests gold and purifies it — and your faith is far more precious to God than mere gold; so if your faith remains strong after being tried in the test tube of fiery trials, it will bring you much praise and glory and honor on the day of his return.

1 PETER 1:7 TLB

PRAYERS

Deliver us from the evil one.

MATTHEW 6:13 NKJV

The Lord will deliver me from every evil work and preserve me for His heavenly kingdom.

2 TIMOTHY 4:18 NKJV

Watch with me and pray lest the Tempter overpower you. For though the spirit is willing enough, the body is weak.

MARK 14:38 TLB

We always pray for you, asking our God to help you live the kind of life he called you to live. We pray that with his power God will help you do the good things you want and perform the works that come from your faith.

2 THESSALONIANS 1:11 NCV

Then...you will bring honor to the name of our Lord Jesus, and he will bring honor to you.

2 THESSALONIANS 1:12 CEV

The Lord is faithful and He will strengthen [you] and set you on a firm foundation and guard you from the evil [one].

2 THESSALONIANS 3:3 AMP

Q: I LOST MY TEMPER — AGAIN. CAN YOU HELP ME, LORD?

A: Those who control their anger have great understanding; those with a hasty temper will make mistakes.

PROVERBS 14:29 NLT

Slowness to anger makes for deep under-standing; a quick-tempered person stockpiles stupidity.

PROVERBS 14:29 THE MESSAGE

INSTRUCTIONS

Put these things out of your life: anger, bad temper, doing or saying things to hurt others, and using evil words when you talk.

COLOSSIANS 3:8 NCV

I promise you that on the day of judgment, everyone will have to account for every careless word they have spoken.

MATTHEW 12:36 CEV

"You're familiar with the command to the

ancients, 'Do not murder.' I'm telling you that anyone who is so much as angry with a brother or sister is guilty of murder.... The simple moral fact is that words kill."

MATTHEW 5:21,22 THE MESSAGE

"Don't sin by letting anger gain control over you." Don't let the sun go down while you are still angry, for anger gives a mighty foothold to the Devil.

EPHESIANS 4:26,27 NLT

When you talk, do not say harmful things, but say what people need — words that will help others become stronger. Then what you say will do good to those who listen to you.

EPHESIANS 4:29 NCV

Let every man be quick to hear, (a ready listener,) slow to speak, slow to take offense and to get angry.

JAMES 1:19 AMP

God's righteousness doesn't grow from human anger.

JAMES 1:20 THE MESSAGE

Do not be overcome by evil, but overcome evil with good.

ROMANS 12:21 NASB

Since God chose you to be the holy people whom he loves, you must clothe yourselves with tenderhearted mercy, kindness, humility, gentleness, and patience. You must make allowance for each other's faults and forgive the person who offends you. Remember, the Lord forgave you, so you must forgive others.

COLOSSIANS 3:12,13 NLT

PROMISES

We have everything we need to live a life that pleases God. It was all given to us by God's own power, when we learned that he had invited us to share in his wonderful goodness. God made great and marvelous promises, so that his nature would become part of us.

2 PETER 1:3,4 CEV

So make every effort to apply the benefits of these promises to your life.... Knowing God leads to self-control. Self-control leads to patient endurance, and patient endurance leads to godliness.

2 PETER 1:5,6 NLT

"Blessed are the merciful, for they shall receive mercy.... Blessed are the peacemakers, for they shall be called sons of God."

MATTHEW 5:7,9 NASB

Delight yourself also in the Lord, and He will give you the desires and secret petitions of your heart. Commit your way to the Lord — roll and repose [each care of] your load on Him; trust (lean on, rely on and be confident) also in Him, and He will bring it to pass. Be still and rest in the Lord; wait for Him, and patiently stay yourself upon Him.... Cease from anger and forsake wrath; fret not yourself; it tends only to evil-doing.... But the meek [in the end] shall inherit the earth, and shall delight themselves in the abundance of peace.

PSALM 37:4,5,7,8,11 AMP

PRAYER

Who can understand his errors? Cleanse me from secret faults. Keep back Your servant also from presumptuous sins; let them not have dominion over me. Then I shall be blameless, and I shall be innocent of great transgression. Let the words of my mouth and the meditation of my heart be acceptable in Your sight, O

Lord, my strength and my Redeemer.

PSALM 19:12-14 NKJV

We always pray that God will show you everything he wants you to do and that you may have all the wisdom and understanding that his Spirit gives. Then you will live a life that honors the Lord.

COLOSSIANS 1:9,10 CEV

EXAMPLE

Our Heavenly Father sees our failures and weakness yet responds with mercy and not anger.

The Lord is merciful and gracious, slow to anger, and plenteous in mercy and loving-kindness. He will not always chide or be contending, neither will He keep His anger for ever or hold a grudge. He has not dealt with us after our sins, nor rewarded us according to our iniquities.... As a father loves and pities his children, so the Lord loves and pities those who fear Him — with reverence, worship and awe. For He knows our frame; He [earnestly] remembers and imprints [on His heart] that we are dust.

PSALM 103:8-10,13,14 AMP

Q: IT'S BEEN A TOUGH DAY, LORD. DO YOU HAVE ANY WORDS OF ENCOURAGEMENT FOR ME?

A: "Do not fear, for I am with you; do not anxiously look about you, for I am your God. I will strengthen you, surely I will help you, surely I will uphold you with My righteous right hand."

ISAIAH 41:10 NASB

Whatever I have, wherever I am, I can make it through anything in the One who makes me who I am.

PHILIPPIANS 4:13 THE MESSAGE

INSTRUCTIONS

Cast your burden upon the Lord and He will sustain you; He will never allow the righteous to be shaken.

PSALM 55:22 NASB

Fix your thoughts on what is true and good and right. Think about things that are pure and lovely, and dwell on the fine, good things in others. Think about all you can praise God for and be glad about. Keep putting into practice all you learned from me...and the God of peace will be with you.

PHILIPPIANS 4:8,9 TLB

Let the peace of heart that comes from Christ be always present in your hearts and lives.... And always be thankful.

COLOSSIANS 3:15 TLB

Let us hold unswervingly to the hope we profess, for he who promised is faithful.

HEBREWS 10:23 NIV

Nothing you do for him is a waste of time or effort.

1 CORINTHIANS 15:58 THE MESSAGE

We fix our eyes not on what is seen, but on what is unseen. For what is seen is temporary, but what is unseen is eternal.

2 CORINTHIANS 4:18 NIV

We live by faith, not by sight.

2 CORINTHIANS 5:7 NIV

Now faith is being sure of what we hope for and certain of what we do not see.

HEBREWS 11:1 NIV

Even though on the outside it often looks like things are falling apart on us, on the inside, where God is making new life, not a day goes by without his unfolding grace.

2 CORINTHIANS 4:16 THE MESSAGE

We are like clay jars in which this treasure is stored. The real power comes from God and not from us. Even when we don't know what to do, we never give up. In times of trouble, God is with us, and when we are knocked down, we get up again. 2 CORINTHIANS 4:7-9 CEV

We felt like we'd been sent to death row, that it was all over for us. As it turned out, it was the best thing that could have happened. Instead of trusting in our own strength or wits to get out of it, we were forced to trust God totally — not a bad idea since he's the God who raises the dead!

2 CORINTHIANS 1:9 THE MESSAGE

PROMISES

And I am sure that God, who began the good work within you, will continue his work until it is finally finished on that day when Christ Jesus comes back again.

PHILIPPIANS 1:6 NLT

Be energetic in your life of salvation, reverent and sensitive before God. That energy is God's energy, an energy deep within you, God himself willing and working at what will give him the most pleasure.

PHILIPPIANS 2:12,13 THE MESSAGE

PRAYERS

We pray that you'll have the strength to stick it out over the long haul...strength that endures the unendurable and spills over into joy.

COLOSSIANS 1:11,12 THE MESSAGE

We wait in hope for the Lord; he is our help and our shield. In him our hearts rejoice, for we trust in his holy name. May your unfailing love rest upon us, O Lord, even as we put our hope in you.

PSALM 33:20-22 NIV

I wait for the Lord, my soul does wait, and in His word do I hope. My soul waits for the Lord more than the watchmen for the morning.... Hope in the Lord; for with the Lord there is lovingkindness, and with Him is abundant redemption.

PSALM 130:5-7 NASB

When You said, "Seek My face," my heart said to You, "Your face, O Lord, I shall seek." I would have despaired unless I had believed that I would see the goodness of the Lord in the land of the living.

PSALM 27:8,13 NASB

The minute I said, "I'm slipping, I'm falling," your love, God, took hold and held me fast. When I was upset and beside myself, you calmed me down and cheered me up.

PSALM 94:18,19 THE MESSAGE

Now to Him who is able to keep you from stumbling, and to make you stand in the presence of His glory blameless with great joy, to the only God our Savior, through Jesus Christ our Lord, be glory, majesty, dominion and authority.

JUDE 24,25 NASB

EXAMPLE

God gave each of us certain "gifts" to keep us aware of our constant need to rely on His strength rather than our own:

Satan's angel did his best to get me down;
what he in fact did was push me to my knees.
No danger then of walking around high and
mighty! At first I didn't think of it as a gift,
and begged God to remove it. Three times I
did that, and then he told me, "My grace is
enough; it's all you need. My strength comes
into its own in your weakness".... It was a case
of Christ's strength moving in on my weakness. Now I take limitations in stride, and with
good cheer.... I just let Christ take over! And
so the weaker I get, the stronger I become.

2 CORINTHIANS 12:7-10 THE MESSAGE

He gives power to the faint and weary, and to
him who has no might He increases strength —
causing it to multiply and making it abound.

ISAIAH 40:29 AMP

---⟨∞⟩---

Q: LORD, I KNOW YOU CAN
HEAL ME, BUT WILL YOU?
WHAT'S MY PART IN THE PROCESS?

---⟨∞⟩---

A: The Lord says, "I will rescue those who love me. I will protect those who trust in my name. When they call on me, I will answer; I will be with them in trouble. I will rescue them and honor them. I will satisfy them with a long life and give them my salvation."

PSALM 91:14-16 NLT

I am the Lord that healeth thee.

EXODUS 15:26 KJV

INSTRUCTIONS

Trust in the Lord with all your heart and do not lean on your own understanding. In all your ways acknowledge Him, and He will make your paths straight. Do not be wise in your own eyes; fear the Lord and turn away from evil. It will be healing to your body and refreshment to your bones. PROVERBS 3:5-8 NASB

Pay attention, my child, to what I say. Listen carefully. Don't lose sight of my words. Let them penetrate deep within your heart, for they bring life and radiant health to anyone who discovers their meaning.

PROVERBS 4:20-22 NLT

Is any one of you sick? He should call the elders of the church to pray over him and anoint him with oil in the name of the Lord. And the prayer offered in faith will make the sick person well; the Lord will raise him up. If he has sinned, he will be forgiven. Therefore confess your sins to each other and pray for each other so that you may be healed. The prayer of a righteous man is powerful and effective.

JAMES 5:14-16 NIV

"These signs will follow those who believe: In My name they will cast out demons...they will lay hands on the sick, and they will recover."

MARK 16:17,18 NKJV

The truth is, anyone who believes in me will do

the same works I have done, and even greater works, because I am going to be with the Father. You can ask for anything in my name, and I will do it, because the work of the Son brings glory to the Father.

JOHN 14:12,13 NLT

God's love, though, is ever and always, eternally present to all who fear him, making everything right for them and their children as they follow his Covenant ways and remember to do whatever he said.

PSALM 103:17,18 THE MESSAGE

Seek the Lord and His strength; seek His face evermore! Remember His marvelous works which He has done, His wonders, and the judgments of His mouth. He remembers His covenant forever, the word which He commanded, for a thousand generations.

PSALM 105:4,5,8 NKJV

Give thanks to the Lord and proclaim his greatness. Let the whole world know what he has done. Sing to him; yes, sing his praises. Tell everyone about his miracles.... O worshipers of the Lord, rejoice!

PSALM 105:1-3 NLT

Never give up praying. And when you pray, keep alert and be thankful.

COLOSSIANS 4:2 CEV

PROMISES

Of all the people on earth, the Lord your God has chosen you to be his own special treasure... He is the faithful God who keeps his covenant for a thousand generations and constantly loves those who love him and obey his commands. He will love you and bless you.... And the Lord will protect you from all sickness.

DEUTERONOMY 7:6,9,13,15 NLT

"I will restore you to health and heal your wounds," declares the Lord.

JEREMIAH 30:17 NIV

He took our suffering on him and felt our pain for us. We saw his suffering. We thought God was punishing him. But he was wounded for the wrong things we did. He was crushed for the evil things we did. The punishment, which made us well, was given to him. And we are healed because of his wounds.

ISAIAH 53:4,5 ICB

Christ carried our sins in his body on the cross. He did this so that we would stop living for sin and start living for what is right. And we are healed because of his wounds.

1 PETER 2:24 ICB

You must worship the Lord your God. If you do, I will bless your bread and your water. I will take away sickness from you. I will allow you to live long lives.

EXODUS 23:25,26 ICB

Jesus said to him, "I will go and heal him."

MATTHEW 8:7 NIV

He sent forth his word and healed them; he rescued them from the grave.

PSALM 107:20 NIV

"Be strong and of good courage, do not fear nor be afraid of them; for the Lord your God, He is the One who goes with you. He will not leave you nor forsake you."

DEUTERONOMY 31:6 NKJV

PRAYERS

What shall I render to the Lord for all His benefits toward me? I will take up the cup of

salvation, and call upon the name of the Lord....
I will offer to You the sacrifice of thanksgiving,
and will call upon the name of the Lord.

PSALM 116:12,13,17 NKJV

Oh my soul, bless God, don't forget a single
blessing! He forgives your sins — every one.
He heals your diseases — every one.

PSALM 103:2,3 THE MESSAGE

Heal me, O Lord, and I will be healed; save
me and I will be saved, for you are the one I
praise.

JEREMIAH 17:14 NIV

Lord, how you have helped me before! You
took me safely from my mother's womb and
brought me through the years of infancy. I have
depended upon you since birth; you have always
been my God. Don't leave me now, for trouble
is near and no one else can possibly help.

PSALM 22:9-11 TLB

I pray that God, who gives peace, will make
you completely holy. And may your spirit, soul,
and body be kept healthy and faultless until
our Lord Jesus returns. The one who chose you
can be trusted, and he will do this.

1 THESSALONIANS 5:23,24 CEV

He is my God, and I am trusting him. For he rescues you from every trap, and protects you from the fatal plague. He will shield you with his wings! They will shelter you. His faithful promises are your armor.

PSALM 91:2-4 TLB

In your day of trouble, may the Lord be with you! May the God of Jacob keep you from all harm. May there be shouts of joy when we hear the news of your victory, flags flying with praise to God for all that he has done for you.

PSALM 20:1,5 TLB

"Whatever you ask for in prayer, believe that you have received it, and it will be yours."

MARK 11:24 NIV

EXAMPLES

There are many examples in the Bible of people asking for — and receiving — healing. Here are three:

As Jesus went on from there, two blind men followed him, calling out, "Have mercy on us, Son of David!" When he had gone indoors, the blind men came to him, and he asked them,

"Do you believe that I am able to do this?"
"Yes, Lord," they replied. Then he touched
their eyes and said, "According to your faith
will it be done to you."

MATTHEW 9:27-29 NIV

A man with leprosy came and knelt before him
and said, "Lord, if you are willing, you can make
me clean." Jesus reached out his hand and
touched the man. "I am willing," he said. "Be
clean!" Immediately he was cured of his leprosy.

MATTHEW 8:2,3 NIV

One of them, when he saw he was healed,
came back, praising God in a loud voice. He
threw himself at Jesus' feet and thanked him
— and he was a Samaritan. Jesus asked, "Were
not all ten cleansed? Where are the other nine?
Was no one found to return and give praise to
God except this foreigner?" Then he said to
him, "Rise and go; your faith has made you
well."

LUKE 17:15-19 NIV

Jesus Christ never changes! He is the same
yesterday, today, and forever.

HEBREWS 13:8 CEV

Q: Lord, I've prayed, but don't see any changes. What should I do now?

A: Trust in the Lord, and do good; dwell in the land, and feed on His faithfulness. Delight yourself also in the Lord, and He shall give you the desires of your heart. Commit your way to the Lord, trust also in Him, and He shall bring it to pass. Rest in the Lord, and wait patiently for Him.

Psalm 37:3-5,7 NKJV

INSTRUCTIONS

You need to persevere so that when you have done the will of God, you will receive what he has promised.

Hebrews 10:36 NIV

Therefore, take up the full armor of God, so that you may be able to resist in the evil day, and having done everything, to stand firm.

Ephesians 6:13 NASB

Stand firm. Let nothing move you. Always give yourselves fully to the work of the Lord, because you know that your labor in the Lord is not in vain.

1 CORINTHIANS 15:58 NIV

Wait...for God. Wait with hope. Hope now; hope always!

PSALM 131:3 THE MESSAGE

"Have faith in God," Jesus answered. "I tell you the truth, if anyone says to this mountain, 'Go, throw yourself into the sea,' and does not doubt in his heart but believes that what he says will happen, it will be done for him. Therefore I tell you, whatever you ask for in prayer, believe that you have received it, and it will be yours."

MARK 11:22-24 NIV

We're not giving up. How could we! Even though on the outside it often looks like things are falling apart on us, on the inside, where God is making new life, not a day goes by without his unfolding grace.... There's far more here than meets the eye. The things we see now are here today, gone tomorrow. But the things we can't see now will last forever.

2 CORINTHIANS 4:16,18 THE MESSAGE

Be like those who through faith and patience will receive what God has promised.

HEBREWS 6:12 NCV

Stay with God! Take heart. Don't quit. I'll say it again: Stay with God.

PSALM 27:14 THE MESSAGE

PRAYERS

May the God of hope fill you with all joy and peace as you trust in him, so that you may overflow with hope by the power of the Holy Spirit.

ROMANS 15:13 NIV

We pray that you'll have the strength to stick it out over the long haul — not the grim strength of gritting your teeth but the glory-strength God gives. It is strength that endures the unendurable and spills over into joy.

COLOSSIANS 1:11 THE MESSAGE

PROMISES

Everything that was written in the past was written to teach us. The Scriptures give us patience and encouragement so that we can have hope. Patience and encouragement come from God.

ROMANS 15:4,5 NCV

He gives power to the faint and weary, and to him who has no might He increases strength — causing it to multiply and making it abound...Those who wait for the Lord — who expect, look for and hope in Him — shall change and renew their strength and power; they shall lift their wings and mount up [close to God] as eagles [mount up to the sun]; they shall run and not be weary; they shall walk and not faint or become tired.

ISAIAH 40:29,31 AMP

Don't worry about anything; instead, pray about everything. Tell God what you need, and thank him for all he has done. If you do this, you will experience God's peace, which is far more wonderful than the human mind can understand. His peace will guard your hearts and minds as you live in Christ Jesus.

PHILIPPIANS 4:6,7 NLT

The earnest (heartfelt, continued) prayer of a righteous man makes tremendous power available — dynamic in its working.

JAMES 5:16 AMP

When God made his promise to Abraham, he backed it to the hilt, putting his own reputation on the line. He said, "I promise that I'll bless you with everything I have — bless and bless and bless!" Abraham stuck it out and got everything that had been promised to him.

When God wanted to guarantee his promises, he gave his word, a rock-solid guarantee — God can't break his word. And because his word cannot change, the promise is likewise unchangeable.

We who have run for our very lives to God have every reason to grab the promised hope with both hands and never let go. It's an unbreakable spiritual lifeline, reaching past all appearances right to the very presence of God.

HEBREWS 6:13,14,17-19 THE MESSAGE

We continue to shout our praise even when we're hemmed in with troubles, because we know how troubles can develop passionate patience in us, and how that patience in turn forges the tempered steel of virtue, keeping us alert for whatever God will do next.

ROMANS 5:3,4 THE MESSAGE

EXAMPLE

Abraham kept believing God's promise to him, no matter what he saw or felt:

There was no hope that Abraham would have children. But Abraham believed God and continued hoping, and so he became the father of many nations. As God told him, "Your descendants also will be too many to count." Abraham was almost a hundred years old, much past the age for having children, and Sarah could not have children. Abraham thought about all this, but his faith in God did not become weak. He never doubted that God would keep his promise, and he never stopped believing. He grew stronger in his faith and gave praise to God. Abraham felt sure that God was able to do what he had promised.

ROMANS 4:18-21 NCV

And so after waiting patiently, Abraham received what was promised.

HEBREWS 6:15 NIV

Q: LORD, I'M HAVING TROUBLE PAYING MY BILLS. DO YOU HAVE ANY ADVICE FOR ME?

A: I will instruct you and teach you in the way which you should go; I will counsel you with My eye upon you.

PSALM 32:8 NASB

"I am the Lord your God, who teaches you to profit, who leads you in the way you should go."

ISAIAH 48:17 NASB

The reward of humility and the fear of the Lord are riches, honor and life.

PROVERBS 22:4 NASB

INSTRUCTIONS

How blessed is the man who fears the Lord, who greatly delights in His commandments.... Wealth and riches are in his house, and his righteousness endures forever.

PSALM 112:1,3 NASB

In everything you do, put God first, and he will direct you and crown your efforts with success.

PROVERBS 3:6 TLB

For the Lord gives wisdom; from His mouth come knowledge and understanding; He stores up sound wisdom for the upright; He is a shield to those who walk uprightly; He guards the paths of justice, and preserves the way of His saints.

PROVERBS 2:6-8 NKJV

The Lord will guide you continually, and satisfy your soul in drought, and strengthen your bones; you shall be like a watered garden, and like a spring of water, whose waters do not fail.

ISAIAH 58:11 NKJV

I have been young and now I am old. And in all my years I have never seen the Lord forsake a man who loves him; nor have I seen the children of the godly go hungry.

PSALM 37:25,26 TLB

"Don't worry about having enough food or drink or clothing. Why be like the pagans who are so deeply concerned about these things? Your heavenly Father already knows all your needs, and he will give you all you need from day to day if you live for him and make the Kingdom of God your primary concern. So don't worry about tomorrow, for tomorrow will bring its own worries. Today's trouble is enough for today."

MATTHEW 6:31-34 NLT

"Don't get worked up about what may or may not happen tomorrow. God will help you deal with whatever hard things come up when the time comes."

MATTHEW 6:34 THE MESSAGE

"This Book of the Law shall not depart from your mouth, but you shall meditate in it day and night, that you may observe to do according to all that is written in it. For then you will make your way prosperous, and then you will have good success.... Be strong and of good courage; do not be afraid, nor be dismayed, for the Lord your God is with you wherever you go."

JOSHUA 1:8,9 NKJV

Lazy hands make a man poor, but diligent hands bring wealth.

PROVERBS 10:4 NIV

The sluggard craves and gets nothing, but the desires of the diligent are fully satisfied.

PROVERBS 13:4 NIV

He who tills his land will have plenty of food, but he who follows empty pursuits will have poverty in plenty.

PROVERBS 28:19 NASB

Lust for money brings trouble and nothing but trouble. Going down that path, some lose their footing in the faith completely and live to regret it bitterly ever after.

1 TIMOTHY 6:10 THE MESSAGE

Don't be obsessed with getting more material things.

HEBREWS 13:5 THE MESSAGE

Keep your lives free from the love of money, and be satisfied with what you have. God has said, "I will never leave you; I will never forget you." So we can be sure when we say, "I will not be afraid, because the Lord is my helper. People can't do anything to me."

HEBREWS 13:5,6 NCV

"You can't worship two gods at once. Loving one god, you'll end up hating the other.

Adoration of one feeds contempt for the other.
You can't worship God and Money both."

MATTHEW 6:24 THE MESSAGE

"But you shall remember the Lord your God,
for it is He who is giving you power to make
wealth, that He may confirm His covenant
which He swore to your fathers, as it is this day."

DEUTERONOMY 8:18 NASB

Honor the Lord by giving him the first part
of all your income, and he will fill your barns
with wheat and barley and overflow your wine
vats with the finest wines.   PROVERBS 3:9,10 TLB

"Bring all the tithes into the storehouse so
there will be enough food in my Temple. If you
do," says the Lord Almighty, "I will open the
windows of heaven for you. I will pour out a
blessing so great you won't have enough room
to take it in! Try it! Let me prove it to you!"

MALACHI 3:10 NLT

PROMISES

For if you give, you will get! Your gift will return
to you in full and overflowing measure, pressed

down, shaken together to make room for more, and running over. Whatever measure you use to give — large or small — will be used to measure what is given back to you.

LUKE 6:38 TLB

Mercy to the needy is a loan to God, and God pays back those loans in full.

PROVERBS 19:17 THE MESSAGE

Good will come to him who is generous and lends freely, who conducts his affairs with justice. Surely he will never be shaken; a righteous man will be remembered forever. He will have no fear of bad news; his heart is steadfast, trusting in the Lord.... In the end he will look in triumph on his foes.

PSALM 112:5-9 NIV

Those who seek the Lord shall not lack any good thing.

PSALM 34:10 NKJV

The blessing of the Lord makes one rich, and He adds no sorrow with it.

PROVERBS 10:22 NKJV

This same God who takes care of me will supply all your needs from his glorious riches, which have been given to us in Christ Jesus.

PHILIPPIANS 4:19 NLT

PRAYERS

"The Lord be magnified, who delights in the prosperity of His servant."

PSALM 35:27 NASB

"Both riches and honor come from You, and You rule over all, and in Your hand is power and might; and it lies in Your hand to make great and to strengthen everyone."

1 CHRONICLES 29:12 NASB

In you, O Lord, I have taken refuge; let me never be put to shame; deliver me in your righteousness. Turn your ear to me, come quickly to my rescue; be my rock of refuge, a strong fortress to save me. Since you are my rock and my fortress, for the sake of your name lead and guide me. Free me from the trap that is set for me, for you are my refuge.

PSALM 31:1-4 NIV

Though I walk in the midst of trouble, you preserve my life; you stretch out your hand against the anger of my foes, with your right hand you save me. The Lord will fulfill his purpose for me.

PSALM 138:7,8 NIV

Q: MY LIES KEEP CATCHING UP
WITH ME, BUT IT'S HARD TO
ALWAYS TELL THE TRUTH.
HOW CAN I QUIT LYING?

A: Lovingly follow the truth at all times —
speaking truly, dealing truly, living truly — and
so become more and more in every way like
Christ.

EPHESIANS 4:15 TLB

INSTRUCTIONS

Be an example...with your words, your actions,
your love, your faith, and your pure life.

1 TIMOTHY 4:12 NCV

Tell your neighbor the truth....When you lie
to others, you end up lying to yourself.

EPHESIANS 4:25 THE MESSAGE

An honest life shows respect for God; a
degenerate life is a slap in his face.

PROVERBS 14:2 THE MESSAGE

Stop lying to each other. You have given up your old way of life with its habits. Each of you is now a new person. You are becoming more and more like your Creator.

COLOSSIANS 3:9,10 CEV

Truth will last forever. But lies last only a moment.

PROVERBS 12:19 ICB

The person who tells lies gets caught; the person who spreads rumors is ruined.

PROVERBS 19:9 THE MESSAGE

Good people will be guided by honesty. But dishonesty will destroy those who are not trustworthy.

PROVERBS 11:3 ICB

These liars have lied so well and for so long that they've lost their capacity for truth.

1 TIMOTHY 4:2 THE MESSAGE

PROMISES

Do any of you want to live a life that is long and good? Then watch your tongue! Keep your lips from telling lies! Turn away from evil and do good. Work hard at living in peace with others.

The eyes of the Lord watch over those who do right; his ears are open to their cries for help. But the Lord turns his face against those who do evil; he will erase their memory from the earth. The Lord hears his people when they call to him for help. He rescues them from all their troubles...from each and every one.

PSALM 34:12-17,19 NLT

If anyone is in Christ, he is a new creation; old things have passed away; behold, all things have become new.

2 CORINTHIANS 5:17 NKJV

God is working in you to make you willing and able to obey him.

PHILIPPIANS 2:13 CEV

PRAYERS

You deserve honesty from the heart; yes, utter sincerity and truthfulness.... Create in me a new, clean heart, O God, filled with clean thoughts and right desires.

PSALM 51:6,10 TLB

You want me to be completely truthful. So teach me wisdom. Take away my sin, and I will be clean. Wash me, and I will be whiter than snow.

PSALM 51:6,7 ICB

We have continued praying for you, asking God that you will know fully what he wants. We pray that you will also have great wisdom and understanding in spiritual things so that you will live the kind of life that honors and pleases the Lord in every way.... God has freed us from the power of darkness, and he brought us into the kingdom of his dear Son.

COLOSSIANS 1:9,10,13 NCV

EXAMPLES

There are many accounts in the Bible of people lying. Notice how each of these lies brought consequences:

Then Peter began to curse. He said, "May a curse fall on me if I'm not telling the truth. I don't know the man." After Peter said this, a rooster crowed. Then he remembered what Jesus had told him: "Before the rooster crows, you will say three times that you don't know me." Then Peter went outside and cried painfully.

MATTHEW 26:74,75 ICB

Now he went in and stood before his master. Elisha said to him, "Where did you go, Gehazi?"

And he said, "Your servant did not go any-where." Then he said to him, "Did not my heart go with you when the man turned back from his chariot to meet you? Is it time to receive money and to receive clothing, olive groves and vine-yards, sheep and oxen, male and female servants? Therefore the leprosy of Naaman shall cling to you and your descendants forever." And he went out from his presence leprous, as white as snow.

2 KINGS 5:25-27 NKJV

Now it was about three hours later when his wife came in, not knowing what had happened. And Peter answered her, "Tell me whether you sold the land for so much?" She said, "Yes, for so much." Then Peter said to her, "How is it that you have agreed together to test the Spirit of the Lord? Look, the feet of those who have buried your husband are at the door, and they will carry you out." Then immediately she fell down at his feet and breathed her last.

ACTS 5:7-10 NKJV

———◈———

Q: I KNOW I NEED TO TAKE A
STAND FOR WHAT IS RIGHT.
BUT HOW CAN I HANDLE
THE PERSECUTION?

———◈———

A: Fear not, for I am with you; be not dismayed, for I am your God. I will strengthen you, yes, I will help you, I will uphold you with My righteous right hand. Behold, all those who were incensed against you shall be ashamed and disgraced.   ISAIAH 41:10,11 NKJV

For the Lord God helps me; therefore have I not been ashamed or confounded; therefore have I set my face like a flint, and I know that I shall not be put to shame.   ISAIAH 50:7 AMP

INSTRUCTIONS

Be an example to the believers with your words, your actions, your love, your faith, and your pure life.   1 TIMOTHY 4:12 NCV

You're blessed when your commitment to God provokes persecution. The persecution drives you even deeper into God's kingdom. "Not only that — count yourselves blessed every time people put you down or throw you out or speak lies about you to discredit me. What it means is that the truth is too close for comfort and they are uncomfortable. You can be glad when that happens — give a cheer, even! — for though they don't like it, I do! And all heaven applauds. And know that you are in good company. My prophets and witnesses have always gotten into this kind of trouble.

MATTHEW 5:10-12 THE MESSAGE

There's trouble ahead when you live only for the approval of others, saying what flatters them, doing what indulges them. Popularity contests are not truth contests.... Your task is to be true, not popular.

LUKE 6:26 THE MESSAGE

For I am not ashamed of the gospel of Christ, for it is the power of God to salvation for everyone who believes.

ROMANS 1:16 NKJV

We work hard and suffer much in order that

people will believe the truth, for our hope is in the living God, who is the Savior of all people, and particularly of those who believe.

1 TIMOTHY 4:10 NLT

Stay away from foolish and stupid arguments, because you know they grow into quarrels. And a servant of the Lord must not quarrel but must be kind to everyone, a good teacher, and patient. The Lord's servant must gently teach those who disagree.

2 TIMOTHY 2:23-25 NCV

"Take into your heart all My words which I will speak to you and listen closely. Go to...the sons of your people, and speak to them and tell them, whether they listen or not."

EZEKIEL 3:10,11 NASB

If people persecute you because you are a Christian, don't curse them; pray that God will bless them.

ROMANS 12:14 NLT

Speak up for the right living that goes along with true Christianity.... And here you yourself must be an example to them of good deeds of every kind. Let everything you do reflect your love of the truth and the fact that you are in dead earnest about it.

TITUS 2:1,7 TLB

Put on the full armor of God, so that when the day of evil comes, you may be able to stand your ground.

EPHESIANS 6:13 NIV

PROMISES

The good man does not escape all troubles — he has them too. But the Lord helps him in each and every one.

PSALM 34:19 TLB

You are of God, little children, and have overcome them, because He who is in you is greater than he who is in the world.

1 JOHN 4:4 NKJV

Fear of man will prove to be a snare, but whoever trusts in the Lord is kept safe.

PROVERBS 29:25 NIV

He Himself has said, "I will never leave you nor forsake you." So we may boldly say: "The Lord is my helper; I will not fear. What can man do to me?"

HEBREWS 13:5,6 NKJV

I give you peace, the kind of peace that only I can give. It isn't like the peace that this world can give. So don't be worried or afraid.

JOHN 14:27 CEV

PRAYERS

Lord, defend me. I have lived an innocent life. I trusted the Lord and never doubted. Lord, try me and test me. Look closely into my heart and mind. I see your love. I live by your truth. I do not spend time with liars. I do not make friends with people who hide their sin. I hate the company of evil people. I have lived an innocent life. So save me and be kind to me.

PSALM 26:1-5,11 ICB

The Lord is my light and my salvation; whom shall I fear? The Lord is the strength of my life; of whom shall I be afraid?

PSALM 27:1 NKJV

If God is for us, who can be against us?

ROMANS 8:31 NKJV

May the God of peace himself make you entirely pure and devoted to God; and may your spirit and soul and body be kept strong and blameless until that day when our Lord Jesus Christ comes back again.

1 THESSALONIANS 5:23 TLB

EXAMPLES

Shadrach, Meshach, and Abednego stood together against tremendous pressure. Because they steadfastly refused to bow down and worship the golden idol, God protected and promoted them:

The fire hadn't touched them — not a hair of their heads was singed; their coats were unscorched, and they didn't even smell of smoke! Then Nebuchadnezzar said, "Blessed be the God of Shadrach, Meshach, and Abednego, for he sent his angel to deliver his trusting servants when they defied the king's commandment and were willing to die rather than serve or worship any god except their own." Then the king gave promotions to Shadrach, Meshach, and Abednego, so that they prospered greatly there in the province of Babylon.

DANIEL 3:27,28,30 TLB

Q: I AM TOTALLY OVERWHELMED
BY MY RESPONSIBILITIES.
HOW CAN I COPE WITH
ALL THIS STRESS?

A: "Do not let your hearts be troubled.
Trust in God; trust also in me.... Peace I leave
with you; my peace I give you. I do not give to
you as the world gives. Do not let your hearts
be troubled and do not be afraid."

JOHN 14:1,27 NIV

Don't fret or worry. Instead of worrying, pray.
Let petitions and praises shape your worries
into prayers, letting God know your concerns.
Before you know it, a sense of God's wholeness, everything coming together for good, will
come and settle you down. It's wonderful what
happens when Christ displaces worry at the
center of your life.

PHILIPPIANS 4:6-8 THE MESSAGE

INSTRUCTIONS

Pile your troubles on God's shoulders — he'll
carry your load, he'll help you out.

PSALM 55:22 THE MESSAGE

"Come to me. Get away with me and you'll
recover your life. I'll show you how to take a
real rest. Walk with me and work with me —
watch how I do it. Learn the unforced rhythms
of grace. I won't lay anything heavy or ill-fit-
ting on you. Keep company with me and you'll
learn to live freely and lightly."

MATTHEW 11:28-30 THE MESSAGE

"What I'm trying to do here is to get you to
relax, to not be so preoccupied with getting, so
you can respond to God's giving. People who
don't know God and the way he works fuss
over these things, but you know both God and
how he works. Steep your life in God-reality,
God-initiative, God-provisions. Don't worry
about missing out. You'll find all your everyday
human concerns will be met.

"Give your entire attention to what God is
doing right now, and don't get worked up

about what may or may not happen tomorrow.
God will help you deal with whatever hard
things come up when the time comes."

MATTHEW 6:31-34 THE MESSAGE

"Here's what I want you to do: Find a quiet,
secluded place so you won't be tempted to role-
play before God. Just be there as simply and
honestly as you can manage. The focus will
shift from you to God, and you will begin to
sense his grace."

MATTHEW 6:6 THE MESSAGE

"This is the resting place, let the weary rest";
and, "This is the place of repose."

ISAIAH 28:12 NIV

PRAYERS

The minute I said, "I'm slipping, I'm falling,"
your love, God, took hold and held me fast.
When I was upset and beside myself, you
calmed me down and cheered me up.

PSALM 94:18,19 THE MESSAGE

You are my hiding place! You protect me from
trouble, and you put songs in my heart because
you have saved me.

PSALM 32:7 CEV

Teach me wisdom.

PSALM 51:6 ICB

We also pray that you will be strengthened with his glorious power so that you will have all the patience and endurance you need. May you be filled with joy, always thanking the Father.

COLOSSIANS 1:11,12 NLT

PROMISES

"I have told you these things, so that in me you may have peace. In this world you will have trouble. But take heart! I have overcome the world."

JOHN 16:33 NIV

I love you, O Lord, my strength. The Lord is my rock, my fortress and my deliverer; my God is my rock, in whom I take refuge. He is my shield and the horn of my salvation, my stronghold.

PSALM 18:1,2 NIV

A thousand may fall at your side, ten thousand at your right hand, but it will not come near you.... If you make the Most High your dwelling — even the Lord, who is my refuge — then no harm will befall you, no disaster will come near your tent. PSALM 91:7,9,10 NIV

No temptation has seized you except what is common to man. And God is faithful; he will not let you be tempted beyond what you can bear. But when you are tempted, he will also provide a way out so that you can stand up under it. 1 CORINTHIANS 10:13 NIV

How blessed the man you train, God, the woman you instruct in your Word, providing a circle of quiet within the clamor of evil.

PSALM 94:12,13 THE MESSAGE

When anxiety was great within me, your consolation brought joy to my soul. PSALM 94:19 NIV

But those who hope in the Lord will renew their strength. They will soar on wings like eagles; they will run and not grow weary, they will walk and not be faint. ISAIAH 40:31 NIV

Because the Sovereign Lord helps me, I will not be disgraced. ISAIAH 50:7 NIV

I can do all things through Christ who strengthens me.

PHILIPPIANS 4:13 NKJV

If you need wisdom — if you want to know what God wants you to do — ask him, and he will gladly tell you.

JAMES 1:5 NLT

Wisdom and truth will enter the very center of your being, filling your life with joy.

PROVERBS 2:10 TLB

EXAMPLE

When Moses was overwhelmed with the responsibility of caring for the nation of Israel, God provided wisdom and a plan that took the pressure off:

"What you are doing is not good. You and these people who come to you will only wear yourselves out. The work is too heavy for you; you cannot handle it alone. But select capable men from all the people...and appoint them as officials over thousands, hundreds, fifties and tens. That will make your load lighter, because they will share it with you."

EXODUS 18:17,18,21,22 NIV

---◇---

Q: I'M LONELY, LORD. CAN YOU HELP ME BUILD LASTING FRIENDSHIPS?

---◇---

A: Love from the center of who you are; don't fake it. Run for dear life from evil; hold on for dear life to good. Be good friends who love deeply.

ROMANS 12:9,10 THE MESSAGE

This is my prayer: that your love will flourish and that you will not only love much but well. Learn to love appropriately. You need to use your head and test your feelings so that your love is sincere and intelligent, not sentimental gush. Live a lover's life, circumspect and exemplary, a life Jesus will be proud of.

PHILIPPIANS 1:9,10 THE MESSAGE

INSTRUCTIONS

Watch what God does, and then you do it, like children who learn proper behavior from their parents. Mostly what God does is love you. Keep company with him and learn a life of love. Observe how Christ loved us. His love was not cautious but extravagant. He didn't love in order to get something from us but to give everything of himself to us. Love like that.

EPHESIANS 5:1,2 THE MESSAGE

Above all, love each other deeply, because love covers over a multitude of sins.

1 PETER 4:8 NIV

Put on a heart of compassion, kindness, humility, gentleness and patience; bearing with one another, and forgiving each other, whoever has a complaint against anyone; just as the Lord forgave you, so also should you. Beyond all these things put on love, which is the perfect bond of unity.

COLOSSIANS 3:12-14 NASB

You must quit being angry, hateful, and evil. You must no longer say insulting or cruel things about others. And stop lying to each other. You have given up your old way of life with its habits. Each of you is now a new person. You are becoming more and more like your Creator.... So be gentle, kind, humble, meek, and patient. Put up with each other, and

forgive anyone who does you wrong, just as
Christ has forgiven you.

COLOSSIANS 3:8-10,12,13 CEV

Give as freely as you have received!

MATTHEW 10:8 NLT

Love endures long and is patient and kind;
love never is envious nor boils over with jeal-
ousy; is not boastful or vainglorious, does not
display itself haughtily. It is not conceited —
arrogant and inflated with pride; it is not rude
(unmannerly), and does not act unbecomingly.
Love [God's love in us] does not insist on its
own rights or its own way, for it is not self-
seeking; it is not touchy or fretful or resentful;
it takes no account of the evil done to it —
pays no attention to a suffered wrong. It does
not rejoice at injustice and unrighteousness,
but rejoices when right and truth prevail. Love
bears up under anything and everything that
comes, is ever ready to believe the best of every
person, its hopes are fadeless under all circumstances and it endures everything [without
weakening]. Love never fails — never fades out
or becomes obsolete or comes to an end.

1 CORINTHIANS 13:4-8 AMP

Gently encourage the stragglers, and reach out
for the exhausted, pulling them to their feet. Be
patient with each person, attentive to individual
needs.... Look for the best in each other, and
always do your best to bring it out.

1 THESSALONIANS 5:14,15 THE MESSAGE

If someone is caught in a sin, you who are spiritual should restore him gently. GALATIANS 6:1 NIV

PROMISES

When the Holy Spirit controls our lives, he
will produce this kind of fruit in us: love, joy,
peace, patience, kindness, goodness, faithfulness, gentleness, and self-control.

GALATIANS 5:22,23 NLT

God has poured out his love into our hearts
by the Holy Spirit, whom he has given us.

ROMANS 5:5 NIV

All who proclaim that Jesus is the Son of God
have God living in them, and they live in
God.... As we live in God, our love grows more
perfect.... We love each other as a result of his
loving us first.

1 JOHN 4:15,17,19 NLT

PRAYER

May the Lord make your love increase and
overflow for each other and for everyone else,
just as ours does for you.

1 THESSALONIANS 3:12 NIV

I pray that the Lord will guide you to be as
loving as God and as patient as Christ.

2 THESSALONIANS 3:5 CEV

We pray that our Lord Jesus Christ and God
our Father will encourage you and help you
always to do and say the right thing.

2 THESSALONIANS 2:16,17 CEV

May your roots go down deep into the soil of
God's marvelous love. And may you have the
power to understand...how wide, how long,
how high, and how deep his love really is. May
you experience the love of Christ, though it is
so great you will never fully understand it.
Then you will be filled with the fullness of life
and power that comes from God.

EPHESIANS 3:17-19 NLT

I pray that your love for each other will overflow more and more, and that you will keep on growing in your knowledge and understanding. For I want you to understand what really matters, so that you may live pure and blameless lives until Christ returns. May you always be filled with the fruit of your salvation — those good things that are produced in your life by Jesus Christ.

PHILIPPIANS 1:9-11 NLT

EXAMPLE

God gave us the ultimate example of love:

This is how God showed his love for us: God sent his only Son into the world so we might live through him.... If God loved us like this, we certainly ought to love each other.

1 JOHN 4:9,11 THE MESSAGE

If we love each other, God lives in us, and his love has been brought to full expression through us.

1 JOHN 4:12 NLT

Q: WHAT SHOULD I LOOK FOR IN A FRIEND?

Pursue faith and love and peace, and enjoy the companionship of those who call on the Lord with pure hearts.

2 TIMOTHY 2:22 NLT

I am a friend to everyone who fears you. I am a friend to anyone who follows your orders.

PSALM 119:63 ICB

INSTRUCTIONS

Whoever spends time with wise people will become wise. But whoever makes friends with fools will suffer.

PROVERBS 13:20 ICB

Stay away from a foolish person. You won't learn anything from him. What makes a person wise is understanding what to do. But what makes a person foolish is dishonesty. Foolish people don't care if they sin. But honest people work at being right with others.

PROVERBS 14:7-9 ICB

Friends come and friends go, but a true friend sticks by you like family

PROVERBS 18:24 THE MESSAGE

The person who shuns the bitter moments of friends will be an outsider at their celebrations.

PROVERBS 14:10 THE MESSAGE

Do a favor and win a friend forever; nothing can untie that bond.

PROVERBS 18:19 THE MESSAGE

When you find a friend, don't outwear your welcome; show up at all hours and he'll soon get fed up.

PROVERBS 25:17 THE MESSAGE

Don't make friends with someone who easily gets angry. Don't spend time with someone who has a bad temper. If you do, you may learn to be like him. Then you will be in real danger.

PROVERBS 22:24,25 ICB

You must not associate with...anyone who calls himself a brother in Christ but who takes part in sexual sin, or is selfish, or worships idols, or lies about others, or gets drunk, or cheats people. Do not even eat with someone like that.

1 CORINTHIANS 5:11 ICB

Do not be fooled: "Bad friends will ruin good habits."

1 CORINTHIANS 15:33 NCV

Don't team up with those who are unbelievers. How can goodness be a partner with wicked-ness? How can light live with darkness? What harmony can there be between Christ and the Devil? How can a believer be a partner with an unbeliever? As God said: "I will live in them and walk among them. I will be their God, and they will be my people. Therefore, come out from them and separate yourselves from them, says the Lord. Don't touch their filthy things, and I will welcome you."

2 CORINTHIANS 6:14-17 NLT

If a fellow believer hurts you, go and tell him — work it out between the two of you. If he listens, you've made a friend."

MATTHEW 18:15 THE MESSAGE

Laugh with your friends when they're happy, share tears when they're down. Get along with each other; don't be stuck-up. Make friends with nobodies; don't be the great somebody.

ROMANS 12:15,16 THE MESSAGE

Become friends with God; he's already a friend with you.

2 CORINTHIANS 5:20 THE MESSAGE

Agree with each other, love each other, be deep-spirited friends.

PHILIPPIANS 2:2 THE MESSAGE

PROMISES

Happy is the person who doesn't listen to the wicked. He doesn't go where sinners go. He doesn't do what bad people do. He loves the Lord's teachings. He thinks about those teachings day and night. He is strong, like a tree planted by a river. It produces fruit in season. Its leaves don't die. Everything he does will succeed.

PSALM 1:1-3 ICB

For wisdom and truth will enter the very center of your being, filling your life with joy. You will be given the sense to stay away from evil men.

PROVERBS 2:10,11 TLB

———❖———

Q: MY FAMILY FIGHTS ALL THE TIME. IS THERE A WAY TO STOP THE STRIFE?

———❖———

A: The servant of the Lord must not be quarrelsome — fighting and contending. Instead he must be kindly to every one and mild-tempered — preserving the bond of peace.

2 TIMOTHY 2:24 AMP

Promote the kind of living that reflects right teaching.... You yourself must be an example to them by doing good deeds of every kind. Let everything you do reflect the integrity and seriousness of your teaching.

TITUS 2:1,6-8 NLT

INSTRUCTIONS

Always be willing to listen and slow to speak. Do not become angry easily.

JAMES 1:19 ICB

When you do things, do not let selfishness or pride be your guide. Instead, be humble and give more honor to others than to yourselves. Do not be interested only in your own life, but be interested in the lives of others.

PHILIPPIANS 2:3 NCV

"Here is a simple, rule-of-thumb guide for behavior: Ask yourself what you want people to do for you, then grab the initiative and do it for them."

MATTHEW 7:12 THE MESSAGE

Don't use bad language. Say only what is good and helpful to those you are talking to, and what will give them a blessing.

EPHESIANS 4:29 TLB

A gentle answer will calm a person's anger. But an unkind answer will cause more anger.

PROVERBS 15:1 ICB

Get rid of all bitterness, rage and anger, brawling and slander, along with every form of malice. Be kind and compassionate to one another, forgiving each other, just as in Christ God forgave you. Be imitators of God, therefore, as dearly loved children and live a life of love.

EPHESIANS 4:31-5:2 NIV

For the whole law can be summed up in this one command: "Love your neighbor as yourself." But if instead of showing love among yourselves you are always biting and devouring one another, watch out! Beware of destroying one another.

GALATIANS 5:14,15 NLT

Do you know where your fights and arguments come from? They come from the selfish desires that make war inside you. You want things, but you do not have them. So you are ready to kill and are jealous of other people. But you still cannot get what you want. So you argue and fight. You do not get what you want because you do not ask God.

JAMES 4:1,2 ICB

Let the peace of Christ keep you in tune with each other, in step with each other. None of this going off and doing your own thing. And cultivate thankfulness.

COLOSSIANS 3:15 THE MESSAGE

Do not do wrong to a person to pay him back for doing wrong to you. Or do not insult someone to pay him back for insulting you. But ask God to bless that person. Do this, because you yourselves were called to receive a blessing.... If you are always trying to do good, no one can really hurt you.

1 PETER 3:9,13 ICB

PROMISES

When a man's ways are pleasing to the Lord, He makes even his enemies to be at peace with him.

PROVERBS 16:7 NASB

Those who are peacemakers will plant seeds of peace and reap a harvest of goodness.

JAMES 3:18 NLT

Work hard at living in peace with others. The eyes of the Lord watch over those who do right, and his ears are open to their prayers. But the Lord turns his face against those who do evil.

1 PETER 3:11,12 NLT

PRAYERS

I pray that God will be kind to you and will let you live in perfect peace! May you keep learning more and more about God and our Lord Jesus.... Do your best to improve your faith. You can do this by adding goodness, understanding, self-control, patience, devotion to God, concern for others, and love. If you keep growing in this way, it will show that what you know about our Lord Jesus Christ has made your lives useful and meaningful.

2 PETER 1:2,5-8 CEV

Now the God of peace.... Make you perfect in every good work to do his will, working in you that which is wellpleasing in his sight, through Jesus Christ.

HEBREWS 13:20,21 KJV

"Love your enemies. Pray for those who hurt you. If you do this, then you will be true sons of your Father in heaven."

MATTHEW 5:44,45 ICB

Here are some examples of that type of prayer:

Jesus said, "Father, forgive them. They don't know what they are doing."

LUKE 23:34 ICB

He [Stephen] fell on his knees and cried out, "Lord, do not hold this sin against them."

ACTS 7:60 NIV

EXAMPLE

Strife between Joseph and his brothers caused great devastation in their family:

Now as it happened, Israel loved Joseph more than any of his other children.... His brothers of course noticed their father's partiality, and consequently hated Joseph; they couldn't say a kind word to him.

GENESIS 37:3,4 TLB

His brothers sold Joseph as a slave, but God was with him and promoted him. Later, Joseph reconciled with his brothers, but only after he tested them to make sure their hearts had changed. (See Genesis 44:18-34).

Then his brothers came and bowed low before him. "We are your slaves," they said. But Joseph told them, "Don't be afraid of me. Am I God, to judge and punish you? As far as I am concerned, God turned into good what you meant for evil. He brought me to the high position I have today so I could save the lives of many people."...And he spoke very kindly to them, reassuring them.

GENESIS 50:18-21 NLT

Q: IS THERE A WAY TO RESTORE CLOSENESS IN A BROKEN RELATIONSHIP?

A: "In repentance and rest is your salvation, in quietness and trust is your strength."

ISAIAH 30:15 NIV

A kind answer soothes angry feelings, but harsh words stir them up.

PROVERBS 15:1 CEV

It is harder to win back the friendship of an offended brother than to capture a fortified city. His anger shuts you out like iron bars.

PROVERBS 18:19 TLB

My dear brothers and sisters, always be willing to listen and slow to speak.

JAMES 1:19 NCV

Listen carefully to what you hear! The way you treat others will be the way you will be treated.

MARK 4:24 CEV

The purposes of a man's heart are deep waters,
but a man of understanding draws them out.

PROVERBS 20:5 NIV

The heart of the discerning acquires knowledge; the ears of the wise seek it out.

PROVERBS 18:15 NIV

Let the wise listen and add to their learning.

PROVERBS 1:5 NIV

Through skillful and godly Wisdom is a house
[a life, a home, a family] built, and by understanding it is established [on a sound and good
foundation]. And by knowledge shall the chambers [of its every area] be filled with all precious
and pleasant riches.

PROVERBS 24:3,4 AMP

When others are happy, be happy with them.
If they are sad, share their sorrow.

ROMANS 12:15 NLT

Stay away from foolish and stupid arguments,
because you know they grow into quarrels. And
a servant of the Lord must not quarrel but
must be kind to everyone, a good teacher, and
patient. The Lord's servant must gently teach
those who disagree.

2 TIMOTHY 2:23-25 NCV

All of you should be of one mind, full of sympathy toward each other, loving one another with tender hearts and humble minds. Don't repay evil for evil. Don't retaliate when people say unkind things about you. Instead, pay them back with a blessing. That's what God wants you to do, and he will bless you for it.

1 PETER 3:8,9 NLT

Be quick to listen and slow to speak or to get angry.

JAMES 1:19 CEV

Let's agree to use all our energy in getting along with each other. Help others with encouraging words; don't drag them down by finding fault.

ROMANS 14:19 THE MESSAGE

Rejoice with those who rejoice; mourn with those who mourn. Live in harmony with one another.

ROMANS 12:15,16 NIV

Confess your sins to each other and pray for each other so that you can live together whole and healed. The prayer of a person living right with God is something powerful to be reckoned with.

JAMES 5:16 THE MESSAGE

He who covers his transgressions will not prosper, but whoever confesses and forsakes his sins shall obtain mercy.

PROVERBS 28:13 AMP

PROMISES

"For I am the Lord your God, who upholds your right hand, Who says to you, 'Do not fear, I will help you.'"

ISAIAH 41:13 NASB

He will turn the hearts of the fathers to their children, and the hearts of the children to their fathers.

MALACHI 4:6 NIV

I will instruct you and teach you in the way you should go; I will counsel you and watch over you.

PSALM 32:8 NIV

"Now then go, and I, even I, will be with your mouth, and teach you what you are to say."

EXODUS 4:12 NASB

PRAYERS

"Teach me, and I will be quiet; show me where I have been wrong."

JOB 6:24 NIV

Show me your ways, O Lord, teach me your paths; guide me in your truth and teach me, for you are God my Savior, and my hope is in you all day long.... He guides the humble in what is right and teaches them his way.

PSALM 25:4,5,9 NIV

EXAMPLES

The older brother of the Prodigal Son is a classic example of an offended person. His father listened, then quietly affirmed his love and concern:

"Look, dear son, you and I are very close, and everything I have is yours. We had to celebrate this happy day. For your brother was dead and has come back to life! He was lost, but now he is found."

LUKE 15:31,32 NLT

When believers withdraw from Jesus, He offers His fellowship and waits patiently for the door to open.

"Look! Here I stand at the door and knock. If you hear me calling and open the door, I will come in, and we will share a meal as friends. I will invite everyone who is victorious to sit with me on my throne."

REVELATION 3:20,21 NLT

—◇—

Q: My parents were critical
of me — and I find myself
being critical of others.
How can I break this cycle?

—◇—

INSTRUCTIONS

Let everything you say be good and helpful, so
that your words will be an encouragement to
those who hear them.

EPHESIANS 4:29 NLT

Say only what helps, each word a gift.

EPHESIANS 4:29 THE MESSAGE

When you talk, do not say harmful things,
but say what people need — words that will
help others become stronger.

EPHESIANS 4:29 NCV

"Be easy on people; you'll find life a lot easier."

LUKE 6:37 THE MESSAGE

Be quick to listen, slow to speak, and slow to

get angry. Your anger can never make things right in God's sight.

JAMES 1:19,20 NLT

There is one who speaks rashly like the thrusts of a sword, but the tongue of the wise brings healing.

PROVERBS 12:18 NASB

"Don't pick on people, jump on their failures, criticize their faults — unless, of course, you want the same treatment. That critical spirit has a way of boomeranging."

MATTHEW 7:1 THE MESSAGE

If you think you can judge others, you are wrong. When you judge them, you are really judging yourself guilty, because you do the same things they do.

ROMANS 2:1 NCV

PROMISES

You shall call, and the Lord will answer; you shall cry, and He will say, Here I am. If you take away from your midst yokes of oppression [wherever you find them], the finger pointed in scorn...and every form of false, harsh, unjust and wicked speaking; and if you pour out that with which you sustain your own life for the hungry, and satisfy the need of the afflicted, then shall your light rise in darkness and your obscurity and gloom be as the noonday.

And the Lord shall guide you continually, and satisfy you in drought and in dry places, and make strong your bones. And you shall be like a watered garden and like a spring of water, whose waters fail not. And your ancient ruins shall be rebuilt; you shall raise up the foundations of...many generations; and you shall be called the repairer of the breach, the restorer of streets to dwell in.

ISAIAH 58:9-12 AMP

The Lord God hath given me the tongue of the learned, that I should know how to speak a word in season to him that is weary: he wakeneth morning by morning, he wakeneth mine ear to hear as the learned.

ISAIAH 50:4 KJV

PRAYERS

"Teach me, and I will hold my tongue; cause me to understand wherein I have erred."

JOB 6:24 NKJV

"I will guard my ways, lest I sin with my

tongue; I will restrain my mouth with a muzzle."

PSALM 39:1 NKJV

Who can understand his errors? Cleanse me from secret faults.

PSALM 19:12 NKJV

Now may the God of peace...Strengthen (complete, perfect) and make you what you ought to be, and equip you with everything good that you may carry out His will; [while He Himself] works in you and accomplishes that which is pleasing in His sight, through Jesus Christ.

HEBREWS 13:20,21 AMP

EXAMPLE

Proverbs 31 gives us a profile of a virtuous woman. When she speaks, her words build up and encourage those around her:

She opens her mouth with wisdom, and on her tongue is the law of kindness.

PROVERBS 31:26 NKJV

Q: YOU WANT ME TO
FORGIVE THEM? AFTER
WHAT THEY DID TO ME?

A: Go ahead and be angry. You do well to
be angry — but don't use your anger as fuel for
revenge. And don't stay angry. Don't go to bed
angry. Don't give the Devil that kind of
foothold in your life.... Be gentle with one
another, sensitive. Forgive one another as
quickly and thoroughly as God in Christ forgave you.
EPHESIANS 4:26,27,32 THE MESSAGE

INSTRUCTIONS

Dear friends, never avenge yourselves. Leave
that to God, for he has said that he will repay
those who deserve it. [Don't take the law into
your own hands.] Instead, feed your enemy if
he is hungry. If he is thirsty give him something to drink and you will be "heaping coals
of fire on his head." In other words, he will feel

ashamed of himself for what he has done to you. Don't let evil get the upper hand but conquer evil by doing good.

ROMANS 12:19-21 TLB

If you forgive men when they sin against you, your heavenly Father will also forgive you. But if you do not forgive men their sins, your Father will not forgive your sins.

MATTHEW 6:14,15 NIV

"If your brother sins, rebuke him, and if he repents, forgive him. If he sins against you seven times in a day, and seven times comes back to you and says, 'I repent,' forgive him."

LUKE 17:3,4 NIV

Make every effort to live in peace with all men and to be holy; without holiness no one will see the Lord.

HEBREWS 12:14,15 NIV

See...that no root of resentment (rancor, bitterness or hatred) shoot forth and cause trouble and bitter torment, and the many become contaminated and defiled by it.

HEBREWS 12:15 AMP

"Do not hate your brother in your heart.

Rebuke your neighbor frankly so that you will not share in his guilt."

LEVITICUS 19:17 NIV

"If another believer sins against you, go privately and point out the fault. If the other person listens and confesses it, you have won that person back."

MATTHEW 18:15 NLT

Brothers, if someone is caught in a sin, you who are spiritual should restore him gently.

GALATIANS 6:1 NIV

All of you should be in agreement, understanding each other, loving each other as family, being kind and humble. Do not do wrong to repay a wrong, and do not insult to repay an insult. But repay with a blessing, because you yourselves were called to do this so that you might receive a blessing.

1 PETER 3:8,9 NCV

Judgment without mercy will be shown to anyone who has not been merciful. Mercy triumphs over judgment!

JAMES 2:13 NIV

A man's wisdom gives him patience; it is to his glory to overlook an offense.

PROVERBS 19:11 NIV

If possible, so far as it depends on you, be at peace with all men.

ROMANS 12:18 NASB

PROMISES

"Do not judge, and you will not be judged. Do not condemn, and you will not be condemned. Forgive, and you will be forgiven."

LUKE 6:37 NIV

God blesses those people who are merciful. They will be treated with mercy!

MATTHEW 5:7 CEV

"Be easy on people — you'll find life a lot easier."

LUKE 6:37 THE MESSAGE

PRAYERS

I pray that God will make you ready to obey him and that you will always be eager to do right. May Jesus help you do what pleases God.

HEBREWS 13:21 CEV

I can do everything with the help of Christ who gives me the strength I need.

PHILIPPIANS 4:13 NLT

EXAMPLE

*Peter asked Jesus, "Lord, how often should I forgive
someone who sins against me?" In response, Jesus
told the parable of "The Unforgiving Servant":*

"The king summoned the man and said, 'You
evil servant! I forgave your entire debt when
you begged me for mercy. Shouldn't you be
compelled to be merciful to your fellow servant
who asked for mercy?' The king was furious
and put the screws to the man until he paid
back his entire debt. And that's exactly what
my Father in heaven is going to do to each one
of you who doesn't forgive unconditionally
anyone who asks for mercy."

MATTHEW 18:32-35 THE MESSAGE

*Jesus gave us the ultimate example in forgiveness
when, as He hung on the cross in terrible pain, He
forgave the very ones who had put Him there:*

Jesus said, "Father, forgive them, for they do
not know what they do."

LUKE 23:34 NKJV

WHAT CAN WE DO TO

Q: MY HUSBAND AND I
ARE HAVING SOME PROBLEMS.
WHAT CAN WE DO TO
IMPROVE OUR MARRIAGE?

A: Be agreeable, be sympathetic, be loving,
be compassionate, be humble. That goes for all
of you, no exceptions. No retaliation. No
sharp-tongued sarcasm. Instead, bless — that's
your job, to bless. You'll be a blessing and also
get a blessing.   1 PETER 3:8 THE MESSAGE

Say only what is good and helpful to those
you are talking to, and what will give them a
blessing.   EPHESIANS 4:29 TLB

Share each other's troubles and problems.

GALATIANS 6:2 TLB

INSTRUCTIONS

"Here is a simple, rule-of-thumb guide for

behavior: Ask yourself what you want people to do for you, then grab the initiative and do it for them."

MATTHEW 7:12 THE MESSAGE

When you do things, do not let selfishness or pride be your guide. Instead, be humble and give more honor to others than to yourselves. Do not be interested only in your own life, but be interested in the lives of others.

PHILIPPIANS 2:3 NCV

Get rid of all bitterness, rage and anger, brawling and slander, along with every form of malice. Be kind and compassionate to one another, forgiving each other, just as in Christ God forgave you. Be imitators of God, therefore, as dearly loved children and live a life of love.

EPHESIANS 4:31-5:2 NIV

Out of respect for Christ, be courteously reverent to one another.

Wives, understand and support your husbands in ways that show your support for Christ. The husband provides leadership to his wife the way Christ does to his church, not by domineering but by cherishing. So just as the church submits to Christ as he exercises such leadership, wives should likewise submit to their husbands.

Husbands, go all out in your love for your wives, exactly as Christ did for the church — a love marked by giving, not getting. Christ's love makes the church whole. His words evoke her beauty. Everything he does and says is designed to bring the best out of her, dressing her in dazzling white silk, radiant with holiness. And that is how husbands ought to love their wives. They're really doing themselves a favor — since they're already "one" in marriage.

EPHESIANS 5:21-28 THE MESSAGE

Honor Christ by submitting to each other.

EPHESIANS 5:21 TLB

Wives, yield to the authority of your husbands, because this is the right thing to do in the Lord. Husbands, love your wives and be gentle with them. COLOSSIANS 3:18,19 NCV

Be good wives to your husbands, responsive to their needs. There are husbands who, indifferent as they are to any words about God, will be captivated by your life of holy beauty. What matters is not your outer appearance — the styling of your hair, the jewelry you wear, the cut of your clothes — but your inner disposition. Cultivate inner beauty, the gentle, gracious kind that God delights in.

The same goes for you husbands: Be good husbands to your wives. Honor them, delight in them. As women they lack some of your advantages. But in the new life of God's grace, you're equals. Treat your wives, then, as equals so your prayers don't run aground.

1 PETER 3:1-4,7 THE MESSAGE

"Don't pick on people, jump on their failures, criticize their faults — unless, of course, you want the same treatment. That critical spirit has a way of boomeranging. It's easy to see a smudge on your neighbor's face and be oblivious to the ugly sneer on your own. Do you have the nerve to say, 'Let me wash your face for you,' when your own face is distorted by contempt?...Wipe that ugly sneer off your own face, and you might be fit to offer a washcloth to your neighbor."

MATTHEW 7:1-5 THE MESSAGE

"Be easy on people; you'll find life a lot easier. Give away your life; you'll find life given back, but not merely given back — given back with bonus and blessing. Giving, not getting, is the way. Generosity begets generosity."

LUKE 6:37,38 THE MESSAGE

"If you give, you will get! Your gift will return to you in full and overflowing measure, pressed down, shaken together to make room for more, and running over. Whatever measure you use to give — large or small — will be used to measure what is given back to you."

LUKE 6:38 TLB

For the whole law can be summed up in this one command: "Love your neighbor as yourself." But if instead of showing love among yourselves you are always biting and devouring one another, watch out! Beware of destroying one another.

GALATIANS 5:14,15 NLT

It is obvious what kind of life develops out of trying to get your own way all the time: repetitive, loveless, cheap sex; a stinking accumulation of mental and emotional garbage; frenzied and joyless grabs for happiness; trinket gods; magic-show religion; paranoid loneliness; cutthroat competition; all-consuming-yet-never-satisfied wants; a brutal temper; an impotence to love or be loved; divided homes and divided lives; small-minded and lopsided pursuits; the vicious habit of depersonalizing everyone into a rival; uncontrolled and uncontrollable addictions; ugly parodies of community. I could go on.

This isn't the first time I have warned you, you know. If you use your freedom this way, you will not inherit God's kingdom.

GALATIANS 5:19-21 THE MESSAGE

Where do you think all these appalling wars and quarrels come from? Do you think they just happen? Think again. They come about because you want your own way, and fight for it deep inside yourselves. You lust for what you don't have and are willing to kill to get it. You want what isn't yours and will risk violence to get your hands on it. You wouldn't think of just asking God for it, would you? And why not? Because you know you'd be asking for what you have no right to. You're spoiled children, each wanting your own way.

JAMES 4:1-3 THE MESSAGE

"In your anger do not sin": Do not let the sun go down while you are still angry, and do not give the devil a foothold.

EPHESIANS 4:26,27 NIV

A man's discretion makes him slow to anger, And it is his glory to overlook a transgression.

PROVERBS 19:11 NASB

Keeping away from strife is an honor for a man, but any fool will quarrel.... A plan in the heart of a man is like deep water, but a man of understanding draws it out.

PROVERBS 20:3,5 NASB

Make this your common practice: Confess your sins to each other and pray for each other so that you can live together whole and healed. The prayer of a person living right with God is something powerful to be reckoned with.

JAMES 5:16 THE MESSAGE

Let the peace of Christ keep you in tune with each other, in step with each other. None of this going off and doing your own thing. And cultivate thankfulness.

COLOSSIANS 3:15 THE MESSAGE

If ye have bitter envying and strife in your hearts, glory not, and lie not against the truth.

This wisdom descendeth not from above, but is earthly, sensual, devilish. For where envying and strife is, there is confusion and every evil work.

JAMES 3:14-16 KJV

Do the hard work of getting along with each other, treating each other with dignity and honor.

JAMES 3:18 THE MESSAGE

Those who are peacemakers will plant seeds of peace and reap a harvest of goodness.

JAMES 3:18 NLT

PROMISES

Lord, you establish peace for us; all that we have accomplished you have done for us.

ISAIAH 26:12 NIV

For he himself is our peace, who has made the two one and has destroyed the barrier, the dividing wall of hostility.

EPHESIANS 2:14 NIV

I can do all things through Christ who strengthens me.

PHILIPPIANS 4:13 NKJV

[Not in your own strength] for it is God Who is all the while effectually at work in you — energizing and creating in you the power and desire — both to will and to work for His good pleasure and satisfaction and delight.

PHILIPPIANS 2:13 AMP

God can do anything, you know — far more than you could ever imagine or guess or request in your wildest dreams! He does it not by pushing us around but by working within us, his Spirit deeply and gently within us.

EPHESIANS 3:20 THE MESSAGE

"If you want a happy life and good days, keep your tongue from speaking evil, and keep your lips from telling lies. Turn away from evil and do good. Work hard at living in peace with others The eyes of the Lord watch over those who do right, and his ears are open to their prayers. But the Lord turns his face against those who do evil."

1 PETER 3:10-12 NLT

No temptation has overtaken you except such as is common to man; but God is faithful, who will not allow you to be tempted beyond what you are able, but with the temptation will also make the way of escape, that you may be able to bear it.

1 CORINTHIANS 10:13 NKJV

The Lord knows how to rescue godly people from their trials.

2 PETER 2:9 NLT

PRAYERS

We pray that you'll have the strength to stick it out over the long haul — not the grim strength of gritting your teeth but the glory-strength God gives. It is strength that endures the unendurable and spills over into joy.

COLOSSIANS 1:11 THE MESSAGE

Now the God of peace...Make you perfect in every good work to do his will, working in you that which is wellpleasing in his sight, through Jesus Christ.

HEBREWS 13:20,21 KJV

With this in mind, we constantly pray for you...that by his power he may fulfil every good purpose of yours and every act prompted by your faith.

2 THESSALONIANS 1:11 NIV

We pray for you all the time — pray that our

God will make you fit for what he's called you to be, pray that he'll fill your good ideas and acts of faith with his own energy so that it all amounts to something. If your life honors the name of Jesus, he will honor you. Grace is behind and through all of this, our God giving himself freely, the Master, Jesus Christ, giving himself freely.

2 THESSALONIANS 1:11,12 THE MESSAGE

EXAMPLE

David and Bathsheba's relationship got off to a bad start: adultery, deception, even murder. Yet, with God's forgiveness, grace, and help, they overcame their problems, and God used their union to bless all the nations of the earth:

A record of the genealogy of Jesus Christ the son of David, the son of Abraham: Abraham was the father of Isaac, Isaac the father of Jacob, Jacob the father of Judah and his brothers...Jesse the father of King David. David was the father of Solomon, whose mother had been Uriah's wife.

MATTHEW 1:1,2,6 NIV

Solomon tells how David and Bathsheba worked

together to teach him God's wisdom:

When I was a boy in my father's house, still tender, and an only child of my mother, he taught me and said, "Lay hold of my words with all your heart; keep my commands and you will live."

PROVERBS 4:3,4 NIV

Listen, my child, to what your father teaches you. Don't neglect your mother's teaching. What you learn from them will crown you with grace and clothe you with honor.

PROVERBS 1:8,9 NLT

Q: LORD, AM I REALLY SUPPOSED TO WAIT UNTIL YOU PICK OUT A MATE FOR ME?

A: Parents can provide their sons with an inheritance of houses and wealth, but only the Lord can give an understanding wife.

PROVERBS 19:14 NLT

The man who finds a wife finds a good thing: she is a blessing to him from the Lord.

PROVERBS 18:22 TLB

INSTRUCTIONS

And the Lord God said, "It isn't good for man to be alone; I will make a companion for him, a helper suited to his needs."

GENESIS 2:18 TLB

Every good thing given and every perfect gift is from above, coming down from the Father of lights.

JAMES 1:17 NASB

Your heavenly Father will give good things to those who ask him!

MATTHEW 7:11 NCV

Remember, your Father knows exactly what you need even before you ask him!

MATTHEW 6:8 TLB

In his heart a man plans his course, but the Lord determines his steps.

PROVERBS 16:9 NIV

We humans keep brainstorming options and plans, but God's purpose prevails.

PROVERBS 19:21 THE MESSAGE

You're blessed when you stay on course, walking steadily on the road revealed by God. You're blessed when you follow his directions, doing your best to find him. That's right — you don't go off on your own; you walk straight along the road he set.

PSALM 119:1-3 THE MESSAGE

PROMISES

The Lord will guide you continually, and satisfy you with all good things.

ISAIAH 58:11 TLB

Delight yourself in the Lord; and He will give you the desires of your heart.

PSALM 37:4 NASB

He is close to all who call on him sincerely. He fulfills the desires of those who reverence and trust him; he hears their cries for help and rescues them.

PSALM 145:18,19 TLB

The Lord gives grace and glory; no good thing does He withhold from those who walk uprightly.

PSALM 84:11 NASB

PRAYER

May he give you the desire of your heart and make all your plans succeed.

PSALM 20:4 NIV

Q: THERE IS SOMEONE I CARE
ABOUT WHO REALLY NEEDS
TO KNOW YOU, LORD.
WHAT SHOULD I DO?

A: Everywhere we go we talk about Christ to all who will listen, warning them and teaching them as well as we know how. We want to be able to present each one to God, perfect because of what Christ has done for each of them.

COLOSSIANS 1:28 TLB

To this end I labor, struggling with all his energy, which so powerfully works in me.

COLOSSIANS 1:29 NIV

INSTRUCTIONS

If anybody asks why you believe as you do, be ready to tell him.

1 PETER 3:15 TLB

When you are with unbelievers, always make good use of the time. Be pleasant and hold

their interest when you speak the message.
Choose your words carefully and be ready to
give answers to anyone who asks questions.

COLOSSIANS 4:6 CEV

Such confidence as this is ours through Christ
before God. Not that we are competent in ourselves...but our competence comes from God.
He has made us competent as ministers of a
new covenant.

2 CORINTHIANS 3:4-6 NIV

The god of this age has blinded the minds of
unbelievers, so that they cannot see the light of
the gospel of the glory of Christ, who is the
image of God.

2 CORINTHIANS 4:4 NIV

I urge, then, first of all, that requests, prayers,
intercession and thanksgiving be made for
everyone.... This is good, and pleases God our
Savior, who wants all men to be saved and to
come to a knowledge of the truth.

1 TIMOTHY 2:1,3,4 NIV

Pray without ceasing.

1 THESSALONIANS 5:17 NKJV

"To open their eyes so that they may turn

from darkness to light and from the dominion of Satan to God, that they may receive forgiveness of sins and an inheritance among those who have been sanctified by faith in Me."

ACTS 26:18 NASB

Now this is the confidence that we have in Him, that if we ask anything according to His will, He hears us. And if we know that He hears us, whatever we ask, we know that we have the petitions that we have asked of Him.

1 JOHN 5:14,15 NKJV

"Behold, I have given you authority to tread on serpents and scorpions, and over all the power of the enemy, and nothing will injure you."

LUKE 10:19 NASB

"And I will give you the keys of the kingdom of heaven, and whatever you bind on earth will be bound in heaven, and whatever you loose on earth will be loosed in heaven."

MATTHEW 16:19 NKJV

PROMISES

"I was found by those who did not seek me; I

revealed myself to those who did not ask for me."

ROMANS 10:20 NIV

For thus says the Lord God, "Behold, I Myself will search for My sheep and seek them out.... I will seek the lost, bring back the scattered, bind up the broken and strengthen the sick."

EZEKIEL 34:11,16 NASB

I will lead the blind by ways they have not known, along unfamiliar paths I will guide them; I will turn the darkness into light before them and make the rough places smooth. These are the things I will do; I will not forsake them.

ISAIAH 42:16 NIV

Those who err in spirit will come to understanding, and those who murmur [discontentedly] will accept instruction.

ISAIAH 29:24 AMP

Thus says the Lord, In an acceptable and favorable time I have heard and answered you, and in a day of salvation I have helped you.... Saying to those who are bound, Come forth; to those who are in spiritual darkness, Show yourselves — come into the light.

ISAIAH 49:8,9 AMP

TO PRAY FOR THE LOST ONE

I...do not cease giving thanks for you, while making mention of you in my prayers; that the God of our Lord Jesus Christ, the Father of glory, may give to you a spirit of wisdom and of revelation in the knowledge of Him. I pray that the eyes of your heart may be enlightened, so that you will know what is the hope of His calling, what are the riches of the glory of His inheritance in the saints, and what is the surpassing greatness of His power toward us who believe.

EPHESIANS 1:15-19 NASB

My response is to get down on my knees before the Father.... I ask him to strengthen you by his Spirit — not a brute strength but a glorious inner strength — that Christ will live in you as you open the door and invite him in.

EPHESIANS 3:14,16,17 THE MESSAGE

We ask God to give you a complete understanding of what he wants to do in your lives, and we ask him to make you wise with spiritual wisdom.

COLOSSIANS 1:9 NLT

And may the God of peace Himself sanctify you through and through — that is, separate you from profane things, make you pure and wholly consecrated to God — and may your spirit and soul and body be preserved sound and complete [and found] blameless at the coming of our Lord Jesus Christ, the Messiah. Faithful is He Who is calling you [to Himself] and utterly trustworthy, and He will also do it [that is, fulfill His call by hallowing and keeping you].

1 Thessalonians 5:23,24 AMP

BIBLE REFERENCES